"Brendan and DeEtte share their personal journeys with love and wisdom. They have given parents creative tools for using prayer. Parents of prodigals will love this book!"

— MARITA LITTAUER, president of CLASServices Inc.;
author of *Getting Along with Almost Anybody*

"The Hope of a Homecoming is a tender and compassionate look into the heart and mind of a parent seeking answers and comfort in the process of parenting a prodigal. The authors have pulled together a resource that will become a classic. I'll be recommending this book to hurting moms in our MotherWise ministry."

— DENISE GLENN, author; speaker; founder of MotherWise

"This dramatic piece demonstrates what it's like to have hope with skin on it. It captures the concept of hope beyond the debris of life and helps me see that just when I am convinced that the world has given up on itself, along comes hope. Praise God!"

— THE REVEREND DR. DAVID G. MCKECHNIE, senior pastor,
Grace Presbyterian Church, Houston, Texas

The HOPE of a HOMECOMING

ENTRUSTING YOUR PRODIGAL
to a SOVEREIGN GOD

BRENDAN O'ROURKE, PH.D.
AND DEETTE SAUER

NAVPRESS◐.

NavPress is the publishing ministry of The Navigators, an international Christian organization and leader in personal spiritual development. NavPress is committed to helping people grow spiritually and enjoy lives of meaning and hope through personal and group resources that are biblically rooted, culturally relevant, and highly practical.

For a free catalog go to www.NavPress.com
or call 1.800.366.7788 in the United States or 1.800.839.4769 in Canada.

© 2003 by Brendan O'Rourke and DeEtte Sauer

All rights reserved. No part of this publication may be reproduced in any form without written permission from NavPress, P.O. Box 35001, Colorado Springs, CO 80935. www.navpress.com

ISBN 978-1-57683-376-6

Cover design by Kelly Noffsinger
Cover photograph from PhotoDisc
Creative Team: Nanci McAlister, Greg Clouse, Jacqueline Eaton Blakley,
         Darla Hightower, Glynese Northam

Some of the anecdotal illustrations in this book are true to life and are included with the permission of the persons involved. All other illustrations are composites of real situations, and any resemblance to people living or dead is coincidental.

Unless otherwise identified, all Scripture quotations in this publication are taken from the the *Holy Bible, New Living Translation* (NLT), copyright © 1996. Used by permission of Tyndale House Publishers, Inc., Wheaton, Illinois 60189. All rights reserved. Other versions used include: the HOLY BIBLE: NEW INTERNATIONAL VERSION® (NIV®), Copyright © 1973, 1978, 1984 by International Bible Society, used by permission of Zondervan Publishing House, all rights reserved; *THE MESSAGE* (MSG). Copyright © 1993, 1994, 1995, 1996, 2000, 2001, 2002. Used by permission of NavPress Publishing Group; *The Living Bible* (TLB), copyright © 1971, used by permission of Tyndale House Publishers, Inc., Wheaton, IL 60189, all rights reserved; the *New King James Version* (NKJV). Copyright © 1982 by Thomas Nelson, Inc. Used by permission. All rights reserved; and the *King James Version* (KJV).

O'Rourke, Brendan, 1948-
   The hope of a homecoming : entrusting your prodigal to a sovereign God
/ Brendan o'Rourke and DeEtte Sauer.
      p.cm.
Includes bibliographical references.
   ISBN 1-56783-376-3
   1. Family--Religious life. 2. Prodigal son (Parable) I. Sauer, DeEtte, 1941- II. Title.
   BF4526.3 076 2003
   248.8'45--dc21   2002015677

Printed in the United States of America
3 4 5 6 7 8 9 10 / 11 10 09 08

CONTENTS

ACKNOWLEDGMENTS

My precious husband and two youngest children have sacrificed so much of their valuable time with me to allow me to create this book. Daniel, I will forever be grateful for your quiet willingness to edit, do the dishes, drive the kids, and hold me when I doubted I could do it. Devin and Chrissy, thanks for the shoulder massages and the sympathetic ears.

Some of my prayer warriors who saw me through the trying times include Johnnie Pennick (my mother), Diane Buonasera, Karen Anderson, Kay Luther, Karla Launhardt, Sabrina Hergert, Sandy Scott, and, of course, my creative visionary friend, DeEtte.

Last, and most important, thanks to my amazing daughters Vanessa and Natalie, who have taught me so much. Thank you both for agreeing to share your stories with others. You are beautiful young women and God has great plans for you. To each of my supporters: I love you! Thanks for helping me to achieve a dream.

To Jesus, the Wonderful Counselor and Prince of Peace: You have carried me when I was weak and walked with me when I was lost. You have taught me how to return to your love again and again. Your unending love is my hope.

Once a prodigal,
Brendan

George, thank you for holding my hand and my heart. I have learned to receive and give largely because of the power, intensity, and constancy of your love. You are my hero, my friend, and my partner. Together we have experienced His splendid abundance. Thanks for love remembered and good-time love to come.

Marla and Layne, I admire your courage in allowing your stories to be told. I appreciate so much the women you are becoming. You are both such remarkable mothers. I am proud of you and I love you more than anything. Kenneth and Steve, thanks for being sons-in-law I could easily love. You are every child's dream of a father.

Carsan, Keaton, Jennifer, and Stephen, you are the beneficiaries of the grace God has bestowed on me. He transformed this prodigal into your devoted Mamée. I commit my life (as He wills) to supporting, teaching, loving, and cheering each of you. You fill up the spaces of my heart.

I am so grateful for my *chosen* sisters, Jerry Wall and Judy Sauer, who know my darkest moods and my deepest secrets and love me anyway. I have never known such unrelenting acceptance. You challenge me, motivate me, correct me, laugh with me, and pray for me.

Special thanks for support and prayer from Mary Peyton Cochran, Stacy King, Euphanel Goad, and the Gervais family.

Thanks to my church, Faith Baptist Mission, and to Pastor Anthony Simmons for your example of kingdom service that truly glorifies God. During the years I waited for my prodigal's return, the "Boys of Glory" Sunday school class occupied my need to mother and gave me the opportunity to serve. These young men continue to capture my energy and my heart.

My deep and lasting friendship with Brendan has led me onto a path I never thought I'd travel. I am privileged to be a part of this project. For years she has shared with me her genius, compassion, humor, and love for our Lord. Now it will be shared with all.

Thanks to my loving Savior, who changed my world by bringing me into His. To God be the glory!

In His splendor,
DeEtte

INTRODUCTION

IT IS NOT THE SAME TO TALK ABOUT BULLS AS IT IS TO BE IN THE BULLRING.
—SPANISH PROVERB

Shortly after he was diagnosed with the cancer that later took his life, television and film star Robert Urich appeared on ABC's *Good Morning America*. At one point he told cohost Diane Sawyer, "This may sound really strange to you, but I thank God for *the privilege of being tested*." What a fascinating concept—viewing trials as a privilege. Urich believed that he discovered his true strengths as he battled terminal cancer. In the interview he shared the Spanish proverb that opened this chapter.

Years ago I (DeEtte) produced a series on bullfighting for television. To get the feel of the sport, I traveled with a bullfighter, Felipe Zambrano, and his entourage throughout Mexico. Caught up in the excitement, I even decided to try my hand as a bullfighter. Having a bull charge me in the ring was the scariest thing I'd ever experienced, though I survived to tell the story.

Bulls are selected on the basis of their bravery, and only those who will give the audience the best show are chosen. One of the problems in selecting a worthy bull is that it cannot be exposed to the ring or the matador prior to the event. So how can the trainers determine the bravery of a bull? They first test the courage of its mother in the ring.

You are in the ring. Your courage is being tested right now. Although your child has a mind of his own and God will deal with him directly, you are a source of bravery for your child. While you wait for your prodigal to repent and return from whatever "far country" he has run to, he needs your prayers. Indeed, you may be the only one who calls upon the forces of the Almighty and enlists His angels to intercede for your lost child, This book is intended to help you fulfill that mission. Along the way you will face your own limitations and weaknesses. We will show you how to pass through those times and not be overcome. We will lay out a path for intercession, a map for recovery, and a reservoir of hope if your child refuses the call. All of these are accomplished through prayer.

Oswald Chambers says it well in his classic devotional *My Utmost for His Highest*:

> The battle is won or lost in the secret places of the will before God. The Spirit of God apprehends me and I am obliged to get alone with God and fight the battle out before Him. Until this is done I will lose every time. *Nothing has any power over the man who has fought the battle out before God and won there* (emphasis added).[1]

When my (Brendan's) daughter started down the prodigal road I desperately searched for anything to help me fight the battle. At the time, Ruth Graham's book *Prodigals and Those Who Love Them*[2] was all I could find. Although her wonderful book gave welcome encouragement, I needed more. Several Christian writers have produced excellent books on the topic since then. But DeEtte and I sensed a need for practical strategies that could carry a parent through each phase of this journey. Having a prodigal child will most certainly test your spiritual strength and endurance. Although it may not always feel like a privilege to be tested, we hope this book will be a worthy companion to help you withstand the tests and increase your faith in the process.

Parents of prodigals are on a parallel journey with their children. We are not on the sideline talking about it; we are in the bullring staring down the scariest opponent imaginable. Prayer is our sword.

May your prayers be powerful,
Brendan and DeEtte

Part One

PRODIGALS *and* PRAYER

Chapter 1

OUR PRODIGALS

IT TAKES BOTH RAIN AND SUNSHINE TO MAKE A RAINBOW.
—VERN MCLELLAN

"I'm losing it!"

Sitting in DeEtte's bedroom choking back tears, I (Brendan) told my longtime friend that my life was unraveling. She'd been there for me through my divorce and remarriage, through starting over with more children at forty-two. I could fall apart in her company because I knew she understood. Her daughters had made mistakes and taken the prodigal path too. They'd given DeEtte her share of disappointment and pain.

We cried together, and then she told me about the prayer she had been praying for her daughters. Thumbing through the well-worn pages of her Bible, she showed me Psalm 90. I hurried over the psalmist's reminders of how short our lives are and how much time we waste on meaningless pursuits. Then my eyes landed on verse 16, in which the writer begs the Lord to make His deeds known to His servants and His splendor to their children. I was familiar with the deeds of the Lord in *my* life, but I hadn't thought much about my children comprehending God's splendor. It's not that I didn't want my children to know what a splendid God we

15

serve — I just hadn't thought of asking God to reveal Himself to my children.

Desperate for help, I decided to take my eyes off the scary events unfolding in my daughter Vanessa's life and instead focus on what could happen if she experienced the magnificence of the Lord. I'm not sure what I expected, but I prayed and DeEtte prayed with me. As we prayed I realized that I hadn't fully been appreciating God's splendor either. I began to recall the amazing ways God had answered prayers in the past. The Lord had brought new hope into my life when I met my husband Dan. He also had renewed Dan's faith and made him a source of strength for me. The Creator of the universe had enabled Dan and me to create two precious children in spite of a previous tubal ligation. Our son Devin frequently refers to the time before he was born as that time "when I was just a prayer" because we've told him about our Sunday school class praying for us to conceive a child. As I focused my heart and mind on the splendor God had shown me, I felt a deep assurance that He would be there for Vanessa too.

Vanessa's journey went deeper into the shadowlands before she reached a turning point. But she did turn around. She faced her failure, sought God's love and forgiveness, and rebuilt her life.

VANESSA'S *and* NATALIE'S *Stories*

Vanessa was abandoned five times. The first was when her birth mother gave her up for adoption, which is how she came into our lives. After four years of infertility, my first husband and I had decided to adopt. Vanessa was so beautiful. Her clear blue eyes, tan skin, and white blonde hair made people in the supermarket smile when I wheeled her down the aisles. She loved people. As soon as she could say a few words she talked to everyone.

When she was five months old I started my doctoral program a hundred miles from home. Mistakenly, I thought that going to school would be compatible with motherhood. I was gone a lot. Although her father and our nanny were loving and very attentive, I believe that my absence was a second abandonment for her.

The third abandonment came quickly on the heels of my doctoral work. When we least expected it, I discovered that I was pregnant. Vanessa's sister, Natalie, was born when Vanessa was two. Within three months of her birth, Natalie was diagnosed with neuroblastoma—cancer of the nervous tissues. She had a kidney removed, radiation on her eye, and chemotherapy for eight months. Vanessa was thrust on the nanny or other family members for more than a year as we focused on Natalie's urgent needs.

Natalie survived and so did Vanessa, but insecurity had taken its toll. Teachers had called Vanessa the "sunshine girl." However, by third grade a learning disability was tarnishing her shine.

The fourth abandonment came when her father and I divorced. She was seven years old and had no inkling that we were unhappy; our life looked fine on the outside. We both remarried within two years and began having more children. Vanessa would never get the attention she needed. There had been too much change and too many competitors.

By ninth grade Vanessa was well on her way to self-defeat. She acted out her depression and hunger for attention, even negative attention. Underachieving, experimenting with drugs, and sneaking out of the house revealed that she was in trouble. I remember sitting in church the night before we put her in residential treatment. Guilt and shame flooded my soul. All I could do was cry. My spiritual friends surrounded me and we prayed. I hated feeling needy, but I was.

Our family had work to do. Therapy helped some, but Vanessa still carried so many wounds. And I just wanted to get on with a happy life. None of her parents liked the strain of rehashing all the old problems.

Our needs conflicted with hers.

One day I was changing the sheets on her bed when I saw something puzzling. Stuck between the bed and the wall was a baby pacifier. She admitted that she sucked on it at night. At fourteen years old, she was regressing all the way back to infancy when she was alone. My heart broke. How could I help this child who never got enough of the secure feeling every child deserves? She was too old for me to treat her like a baby.

She resolved the dilemma by getting pregnant. When she was seventeen she started her senior year of high school married and expecting a child on Christmas Eve. Her husband, only one year older, enlisted in the army. They went to Germany and tried to be a family for three years. When they returned to the United States her husband left her. Abandoned again, Vanessa fell into the pit of depression, refused to get help, and ended up homeless. She lost custody of her son because she lived with drug dealers and could not even support herself. Vanessa hit bottom. That's when I turned to my friend DeEtte.

Natalie's rebellion was less obvious. Unlike Vanessa, she looked like a normal, high-functioning youth with lots of friends and accomplishments. She did well in school, made cheerleader, and went to church occasionally. Vanessa and Natalie accepted Christ and were baptized and confirmed, but Natalie disclosed later that she felt she had no choice. We discovered after the fact that Natalie drank and smoked a lot throughout high school. In college, she rejected worship or any other organized Christian activity. Her prodigal behavior was subtle, not straying too far but clearly denying the importance of a relationship with Christ. I felt confused and frustrated by her attitude. When both my daughters rejected the values I wanted for them, I didn't know what to do. It was hard not to personalize their problems. My strength and hope had to come from God.

MARLA'S *and* LAYNE'S *Stories*

In the extreme August heat of west Texas, George and I (DeEtte) unloaded a full-to-overflowing U-Haul truck and helped our youngest daughter, Layne, set up housekeeping six hundred miles from home. We weren't supportive when she first announced her plans to move to a barren desert community across the state. We did everything we could to dissuade her, but she was firm in her decision to pursue a career opportunity. I wished we could have been more encouraging.

The distance in miles wasn't all that separated us. Over the past years we watched helplessly as our daughters moved further and further away from the committed young people they had been. The world had seduced them. Every time they rejected our urges to "pray about that," or "come to church with us," or " read this," we felt a deep sadness. To see their eyes roll upward each time we mentioned the Lord was torment.

Just after George and I returned to Houston, the phone rang. It was a close friend urging me to read Psalm 90. When I got to verse 16, the words leaped off the page and into my heart: "May your deeds be shown to your servants, your splendor to their children" (NIV). Those words became mine.

I shouted, "That's it!" I knew what God wanted me to do. I began to pray, "Lord, show them Your splendor." Sometimes it was a request, sometimes a plea, and sometimes a cry from the depths of my soul. I knew God had given me this prayer, this hope.

Years earlier we had experienced the agony of losing Jennifer, our oldest daughter, in a car accident when she was eighteen. Intense grief left us inconsolable, clinging to our two other children. Marla, our middle daughter, began to show signs of rebellion in college. She partied too much, switched schools, and eventually dropped out for a while. Her boyfriend relationships failed. At a time when George and I were beginning to mature spiritually, Marla turned her back on our values. We lost her, not by an auto accident, but by her choice. I cried in my sleep and I cried awake as I pictured Jennifer curled up in the arms of her heavenly Father, protected and safe. Now, I saw Marla running from Him toward danger.

For several years she avoided us. When we were together she was uncomfortable, so she limited the contact. The relationship was strained. She seemed to self-destruct on a regular basis until she began the long path home to the faith of her adolescence.

When I began praying Psalm 90:16 for Layne and Marla, I knew God had to work a few miracles before that prayer would be answered. But I prayed, "Lord, show them Your splendor." I knelt, bowed, sang, read, and prayed some more. Most of all, I trusted Him. And then, the same peace I'd felt the night of Jenny's death washed over me. In the midst of the anguish I experienced joy. My spirit quieted. I knew God was faithful.

Chapter 2

WHO IS A PRODIGAL?

FOR THIS SON OF MINE WAS DEAD AND HAS NOW RETURNED
TO LIFE. HE WAS LOST, BUT NOW HE IS FOUND.
— LUKE 15:24

It was a perfect day for a wedding. The weather was beautiful and the yachts on the bay were at full sail parading past the restaurant window. Gentle love songs played as everyone awaited the bride's entrance. The bridal party entered, and Frank felt his stomach knot as he thought about the array of young people standing in front of him. One of the bridesmaids was just out of rehab for overdosing on a designer drug. Another battled a severe eating disorder; the bridesmaid's dress hung from her skeletal frame. Several of the boys had been in serious trouble, picked up by police on different charges. All had problems with school.

Frank was a close friend of the groom's family, but he felt more disappointed than joyful for the young couple about to marry. Allison, the bride, was eighteen. Her groom was nineteen. In spite of the beautiful clothes and surroundings, sadness accompanied the event. The bride and groom weren't prepared for marriage. God was an afterthought in this major decision of their lives.

Allison was six months pregnant.

These were not young people statistically doomed to failure. They came from upper-middle class suburban families. Fresh-faced, attractive, and intelligent, many of the kids had been churched since infancy. Most were from two-parent families. Frank studied the young people in front of him, and he had an alarming thought: *Every child in America is high-risk.* Every child has the potential of being a prodigal at some time in her life.

Prodigal: A STRANGE NAME

The word *prodigal* is not actually used in Scripture, yet the story recorded in Luke 15:11-32 is one of the most familiar parables in the Bible. Most Bible translations call it The Parable of the Lost Son. Jesus used the parable to teach us how important we are to God—the Father. He wanted us to know that no matter how far we run from Him, He will wait for us and rejoice when we return. The term *prodigal* has become synonymous with the choices made by the son in the parable. He turned his back on God, left his family's values, and wasted his blessings.

In his book *Loving a Prodigal,* Norm Wright explains that the Hebrew words to describe a prodigal include three interpretations. One is the word for "fool," meaning "thickness." A second translation is "lacking foresight," meaning "a tendency to make wrong choices because of having never matured." The third translation is "empty-headed." This interpretation refers to someone who "doesn't have a sense of right and wrong."[1]

When we told our nonChristian friends that we were writing a book for parents of prodigals, they typically responded with "Huh?" Calling a person "prodigal" seems old-fashioned in this mobile, constantly changing era when families move at least five times on average and young people are not taught to be loyal or respectful. Change and self-centered behavior are the world's norm. Christian parents aspire to a greater goal. We want our children to cherish the gifts God has given them, not waste them. Most importantly, we want our children to live their lives in the center of God's will.

But whether we use the word *prodigal* or more contemporary terminology like *defiant, rebellious,* or *out-of-control,* the impact such a child has on his family is powerful. Hope and fear collide as parents seek to cope, intercede, and help their prodigal return.

Can PARENTS Make a DIFFERENCE?

Robert Brooks and Sam Goldstein, highly respected faculty at Harvard Medical School and the University of Utah, respectively, recently wrote a book titled *Raising Resilient Children,* in which they propose that parents *can* help their children handle life's challenges and threats without losing their values. They cite a *USA Today*/CNN/Gallup poll stating that "most parents concur that it is much more difficult today to raise children to be 'good people' than it was twenty years ago. . . . Two out of three parents feel they are doing a 'worse job.' . . . Many hold out changing the world around them as the place in which the solution lies, yet feel overwhelmed with the daunting task of having an impact on a world moving at Mach speed." Brooks and Goldstein go on to say, "We can no longer afford the luxury of assuming that if our children don't face significant stress or adversity they will turn out fine."[2] Unfortunately, Christian parents face the same problems.

The father in the Parable of the Lost Son was a good father. Jesus gives the impression that he hadn't made mistakes with his son. In fact, he appears strong and loving, representing God's attitude toward mankind. The message is not about parents who've failed their children. It is about a child who chooses to act in self-destructive ways. Although parents certainly influence the development of their children, you may not be able to prevent one of them from becoming a prodigal.

What CHARACTERIZES *a* PRODIGAL?

Quin Sherrer and Ruthanne Garlock ask and answer the question, "What produces a prodigal?" in their book *Praying Prodigals Home*. They list three elements that influenced the younger son in Jesus' parable:

- Impatience
- Selfishness
- A desire for adventure[3]

Those three characteristics describe almost every young person in America (and a few older ones, too). Everyone is selfish and impatient at times. And wanting adventure is certainly not bad.

Our definition is a little tighter. We believe two criteria are necessary to warrant the label *prodigal:*

- A willingness to reject God
- A willingness to pursue one's desires regardless of who may be hurt in the process

Notice that the word *will* is part of each criterion. Your child has a choice whether to act out his impulses or to obey God. God gives him that choice. Pastor-teacher James MacDonald of *Walk in the Word* says, "Once you belong to God you only have two choices: obedience or misery."[4] Whether he realizes it or not, the prodigal chooses misery. Or at least he is willing to risk it.

To distinguish a prodigal from others who exhibit rebellious traits in less destructive ways, listen to the prodigal son's words to his father upon his return in Luke 15:21: "Father, I have sinned *against heaven and against you*" (NIV, emphasis added).

Prodigals come in all shapes and sizes. They may be preteens or middle-aged. They may have run to a "faraway land" or live in a bedroom down the hall. They may be rich or poor or anything in between. They may have one parent, two parents, or any number of combinations for blended families. A prodigal's behavior can range from rebellious to blasphemous. Some young people go through a brief, mildly prodigal time in their lives but manage a "spontaneous remission" of symptoms.

By the way, prodigals' parents come in all shapes and sizes too. Many parents of prodigals are godly, loving parents who are completely baffled by their child's behavior. Others were prodigals themselves.

Basically, a prodigal is anyone who knows God but rejects intimacy with Him. Anyone who insists on controlling her own destiny in spite of the consequences could be called a prodigal. God extends to each of us an opportunity for guidance and closeness to Him, but He requires obedience in return. The prodigal refuses the offer.

WHY?

Prodigals reject God's offer because they have a distorted view of God and of themselves. Rather than seeing God as trustworthy, prodigals won't let Him in. They defend the innermost parts of their being from everyone. They fear being hurt or controlled by another— including, and sometimes especially, God. Insecurity and unmet needs drive the prodigal to anxiously seek quick solutions instead of taking the long way around, the way of growth and maturity.

Rebellious behavior may begin as simple defiance or impulsivity, but before long a repeated pattern of resistance to help and refusal to be in relationship marks the life of the prodigal. At that point a parent must fight for the life of her child by drawing the most powerful weapon of all: *prayer.*

Chapter 3

WHAT KIND OF PRAYERS MAKE A DIFFERENCE?

WHENEVER YOU PRAY FOR SOMETHING, YOU MUST TAKE INTO ACCOUNT
TWO ASPECTS OF YOUR REQUEST. YOU MUST CONSIDER
BOTH ITS DIFFICULTIES AND ITS NATURE.
—JOHN WHITE

Isn't one prayer as effective as the next? Maybe. Maybe not. Praying for our children is certainly not a new idea. Parents have prayed for their children throughout history. As Moses' mother quietly slipped him into the Nile, she entrusted her son to divine intervention. We don't know what she prayed, but we know that she trusted God. In spite of the difficulties, she courageously interceded for her son.

Although you can pray for your prodigal in many ways, five specific kinds of prayers worked best for us and for other parents we've interviewed. They are:

- Prayers from a surrendered heart
- Faith-building prayers
- Persistent prayers
- Written prayers
- Shared prayers

The outcomes surprised us. Of course, we wanted our daughters to return to a strong faith, but we had no idea our own faith would be transformed as well.

PRAYERS *from a* SURRENDERED HEART

Joni sobbed, her chest heaving, breath fighting to escape the clutching in her throat. Every time she tried to stop, another wave of agony crashed inside. She sat in my (Brendan's) office apologizing for the uncontrollable burst of emotion. To respect the depth of her feelings, I told her to take her time.

Joni's seventeen-year-old son, Jason, had driven the family car from Houston to Oklahoma after telling his mother that he was going to a weekly drug recovery program meeting. When the Oklahoma state police stopped him for speeding, his name appeared as a missing person in a "stolen vehicle" and they took him into custody. Jason expected his parents to bail him out, but they decided not to rescue him. Jason's life was a mess. Two years of drug abuse, promiscuity, lies, and school failure had worn his family down. His parents were strong Christians who sang in the praise band at church. Jason played guitar and sang with them. They looked like a happy, well-adjusted family until Jason shattered the myth.

Joni kept a strong façade during those years when she couldn't admit what Jason was doing. She sought counseling for Jason, tried tough love, and prayed a lot of desperate prayers. The morning the Oklahoma police called to tell her that her son was in jail, the Lord spoke to Joni in the quiet of her bedroom. He asked her to give Jason to Him, like Abraham gave Isaac. In a still, small voice He whispered, "Give up your child and come closer to me." Joni sat there stunned.

She couldn't give up her child. A Christian mother wouldn't do that. Jason needed her. "Give him up, Lord?"

"Yes, Joni, give him up."

"Why, Lord?"

"Because I want you to grow. You can't grow without surrendering."

"Surrendering?"

"Yes, surrendering."

"Surrendering what, Lord?"

"Your heart."

As she wept in my office, Joni related her conversation with the Savior. He wanted total surrender—not an easy feat. Her heart had been full of fear and resentment for all the trials Jason had imposed on her life. She felt heavy with shame. The tears flowed like welcome rain, washing away the brittle mask she'd hidden behind so long. She slipped onto the floor and knelt. I knelt with her. "Lord, I give Jason to You. He is Yours. If he never comes home or if he never trusts You again, I will trust that You are a sovereign God. I will trust that You care about us. *I want a relationship with You more than I want Jason home.* Let me be Your servant and do Your will."

The drive from Oklahoma back to Texas with Jason sitting in silence might have been filled with lecturing, screaming, or anxiously planning the consequences. Instead, peace filled the car. No words were needed. Joni's heart was freed from pressure. She had no map for the journey ahead, but she knew the Mapmaker would show them the way. Her heart had changed and Jason sensed the difference.

The first step toward bringing our prodigals home is to surrender our hearts and minds to the God of Abraham. Surrender is obedience to God's direction. He must have our full cooperation and we must be willing to let Him stretch our faith.

FAITH-BUILDING *Prayers*

Prodigals test our faith. They shatter everything we trust and expect about them. Fear and inadequacy make us wonder whether God is really there, especially when our prayers aren't answered quickly. Even though Scripture teaches us that He is always present, bearing up under the present reality takes strength.

Prayer strengthens our faith muscles. We need the kind of faith that enables us to boldly march up to the throne of the Mighty God and tell Him what is on our hearts. We must be on a first-name basis with Jesus, the One whose Father ached as the world betrayed Him. Jesus knows what we are experiencing. He's seen it from both sides. Wherever He leads us, we can trust Him.

Faith is difficult if you feel abandoned. That's the reason you must seek communion with God every day and not allow the Enemy to gain the slightest foothold in your thoughts. Satan delights in confusing you. He wants to convince you that God doesn't care and that maybe it's His fault you are suffering. If the Enemy can create doubts, he can eventually plant the weedlike roots of fear where you might have grown an orchard of fruit-bearing trees.

I (Brendan) met a woman recently who told me she had four children. When I invited her to tell me about them, she launched into colorful descriptions of the youngest son who just graduated from high school, the daughter who was a cat-loving accountant living in Chicago, another daughter who would be married in a few months to her high school sweetheart, and then she said, "And I have a son who is going into the ministry." A strange, impish little smile crept across her face as she made this last statement. Taking the bait, I said, "Why do you smile like that when you talk about him?" She blushed and replied, "You see, right now Jack doesn't know that he's going to be a minister. He's been battling depression for a long time and hasn't been able to hold a job for very long. But the Lord told me that He has plans for Jack. I know someday Jack will hear Him too. And when he does, Jack's going to be a heck of a minister." What faith!

This praying, believing mother reminded me of the apostle Paul's words:

> For though we live in the world, we do not wage war as the
> world does. The weapons we fight with are not the weapons of
> the world. On the contrary, they have *divine power to demolish
> strongholds.* We demolish arguments and every pretension that
> sets itself up against the knowledge of God, and we take captive
> every thought to make it obedient to Christ. (2 Corinthians
> 10:3-5, NIV, emphasis added)

Depression is one of the most insidious strongholds Satan uses to
remove us from the knowledge of God. As your mood shifts into low
gear, you slow down and stop reading the Word or stop having fellowship with other believers. You lose the energy and hope that lubri-
cate your spirit and keep you moving forward. The easy, self-centered
escapes like sleep, television, alcohol, and other mind-numbing
excesses become acceptable. Before long, you forget what it feels like
to breathe deeply, to smile, and to know that God cares. All you can
do is cry out for help.

In his book *Wisdom for the Way*, Chuck Swindoll writes, "The
wisdom of God gives us balance, strength, and insight. None of
these is a natural trait. Each is a by-product of wisdom. We don't get
these things just because we're human beings. They must come
from God." He adds, "When we operate in the sphere of the wisdom of God, when it is at work in our minds and in our lives, we
look at life through lenses of perception, and we respond to it in
calm confidence. There's a remarkable absence of fear."[1] If you pray
for wisdom you can conquer fear. Wisdom lets you know that there
is always a way out of any depressing or scary situation. Faith is built
by the knowledge that God will find a way for you to pass through
troubled waters and not be overcome (see Isaiah 43:2).

As hurting, scared parents we encounter many problems.
Oswald Chambers wrote in *My Utmost for His Highest*, "Any problem that comes between God and myself springs out of disobedience—any problem that is alongside me while I obey God increases

my ecstatic delight as I rely on the confidence of God."[2] Faith will empower you to enjoy the confidence of God as you seek to implement His plan for bringing your prodigal home.

You can increase your faith by humbly admitting when you don't have faith. Tell the Lord that you want to believe that He is at work in your and your child's lives, but you don't feel His presence. Get on your knees. Imagine God the Father cupping your face in His powerful but gentle hands as He looks into your soul. He loves you. The Creator knew you before you were born. Look at Him. See the compassion in His eyes. Admit your failures and weaknesses, then tell Him you need His help. Ask for wisdom and courage. Now sit quietly and listen as His Holy Spirit breathes on you, surrounding you with the invisible forces of heaven and filling you with renewed strength and truth. Let faith be your shield. You are ready to face the day.

➤PERSISTENT *Prayers*

Parents of prodigals would do well to memorize the words of the Old Testament prophet Samuel, who once told the people of Israel, "As for me, far be it from me that I should sin against the Lord by failing to pray for you" (1 Samuel 12:23, NIV).

Living by faith means not giving up. Parents who've been embarrassed, depleted, and discouraged find that giving up seems so easy. Persisting in your faith and in your prayers is hard. Yet you must.

In Luke 18:1-8, Jesus told His disciples the parable of a persistent widow who kept pleading her cause before the local judge until he finally gave in and granted her request. He told them this story to show them that they should "always pray and not give up" (verse 1, NIV). God is in the transformation business, and He knows what He is doing. Jesus taught that transformation requires perseverance. When you persistently pray for your child's transformation, you are changed too.

A friend once pointed out how silly it is to think that God doesn't know what's happening in our lives. She told the story of a woman in her Bible study class who was praying aloud for her aunt who had suffered a stroke. The woman began by saying, "Lord, Aunt Tina is sick. She's in room 207 at Methodist Hospital." The friend barely held back a chuckle as she pictured God slapping His forehead and proclaiming, "What! Tina's in the hospital? How did I miss that?" Obviously, our sovereign Lord knows everything. We do not pray to inform Him. We pray to enlist and direct His power toward the matters on our hearts. Throughout the Old and New Testaments we are instructed to pray without ceasing, to pray frequently each day, to pray all night, and so on. That's persistence.

Persistent prayer does not mean that you endlessly repeat the same prayer or that you spend hours on your knees. Always praying means frequently and continually letting God know your concern about your family. It also means returning over and over again to a posture of submission. Whether you are driving in your car or writing in your prayer journal, lift up your requests. Name the people you are concerned about. Ask for wisdom. Even when your prodigal runs the other way, plead his case before Christ. Believe that answers will come, and they will.

Mother Teresa said that she was able to minister to the poorest of the poor because she prayed at least a half-hour in the morning and an hour each night. She said, "Work doesn't stop prayer and prayer doesn't stop work. It requires only that small raising of the mind to Him. 'I love You, God. I trust You. I believe in You. I need You now.' Small things like that. They are wonderful prayers."[3]

Persistent prayers are not moved by the winds of adversity. Like a tree planted firmly on the shore, let your prayers take root just as the prophet Jeremiah describes:

> But blessed are those who trust in the LORD and have made
> the LORD their hope and confidence. They are like trees

planted along a riverbank, with roots that reach deep into the water. Such trees are not bothered by the heat or worried by long months of drought. Their leaves stay green, and they go right on producing delicious fruit. (Jeremiah 17:7-8)

WRITTEN *Prayers*

"Mom, can I come home for a few days?" My (DeEtte's) twenty-four-year-old daughter's voice quivered as she spoke into the phone. Immediately, I told her, "Of course, Layne. What's wrong?" Hesitating for a moment, she said, "We'll talk when I get there." After a hurried goodbye we hung up. I felt confused and worried.

Layne coached a Dallas swim team. She had recently been named North Texas Coach of the Year. I was so proud of her accomplishments. Even more thrilling was the fact that she had rededicated her life to the Lord. Now she was very serious about her faith commitment, and her life showed it. She and her fiancé attended church, went to premarital seminars, and began to focus their social life around Christian friends. We agreed to help plan a spring wedding.

Years before, I had begun a serious, prayerful quiet time. Each morning I spent time nestled in a chair in Layne's old bedroom, reading Scripture, devouring devotional books, singing, and praying over my lengthening prayer list. Most of all I prayed for my two daughters. I recorded my thoughts and insights in a small cloth-bound prayer journal. God guided me to many wonderful truths. He fed me morsels of wisdom, filling me, nourishing me. I had no idea that my journal would become a gift.

When Layne arrived, her eyes were red and swollen. She'd been crying for hours. Her fiancé had broken their engagement. I had never seen her so ravaged by hopelessness. Nothing I could say mattered, so I sat and listened as she spat out words between sobs. Finally, I pieced together the story of how the man she loved had begun to resent all the changes. He wanted the "old Layne" who partied till dawn and slept late on Sundays. He gave her an ultimatum—God or him. She chose God.

The next morning Layne left the house while I was taking my daily walk. When she returned, her magnificent mane of golden brown curls, which had been her most striking feature, was gone. Throwing her head back, she announced with a smile, "I'm starting over!"

That afternoon we sat together and I shared my journal with her. She witnessed the comfort and wisdom I had found while praying for her. I think it gave her strength to go on and faith to wait with anticipation for the man God had chosen for her, the one who would eventually become her husband.

The next Mother's Day Layne sent me the most meaningful gift I've ever received. On a lovely note card she wrote: *I have no greater joy than to hear that my children are walking in the truth (3 John 4, NIV).* I cried tears of gratitude as I copied it into my journal.

Most of us resist writing our thoughts and prayers. The reasons range from fear of exposure to a self-conscious sense of inadequacy induced by some critical, red-pen-wielding English teacher back in our high school days. If we push past the resistance, the reward is worth the angst. Not only does it give us a chance to review where we've been, but it also reminds us of the answers we've received along the way. Hope and faith increase when we read the evidence of God's work in our own lives.

SHARED *Prayers*

Jesus told His disciples, "Again, I tell you that if two of you on earth agree about anything you ask for, it will be done for you by my Father in heaven. For where two or three come together in my name, there am I with them" (Matthew 18:19-20, NIV).

Shame and embarrassment threaten to cut you off from spiritual friends who could pray with you for your child and your family. You fear that others will back away or look down on you if they know the truth about your prodigal—and some might. A greater shame, however, would be missing the opportunity to claim the Lord's promise you just read from Matthew 18:19-20.

The most powerful weapon in the arsenal of a praying parent is the combined Spirit-led prayers of caring friends. As Bruce Larson writes:

> The truth is that a good many of our personal problems could be put in perspective, if not solved, by getting involved with other people's pain. Without this involvement a lot of people wind up materially successful, but unhappy and lonely. Tennessee Williams, who often dealt with the problems of loneliness and alienation in his plays, wrote, "If loneliness is as prevalent as we are led to believe that it is, then surely the great sin of our time must be to be lonely alone." That loneliness can be assuaged only as we reach out for our brother by praying for him, standing with him, weeping when he weeps, and rejoicing when he rejoices. In other words, caring for him as best we can.[4]

Have you ever felt as if you were utterly alone with pain and worry for your child? Perhaps you tried to share your story with Christian friends and they didn't "get it." Maybe they had not yet faced threatening challenges to their family or their faith and were not spiritually mature enough to help. Or maybe your story scared them too much because they had children who showed signs of becoming a prodigal.

You may have to sort through your list of Christian friends to discover the true prayer warriors who do not condemn or shun you. You must recognize which ones may mean well but are actually toxic. Be selective as you build a prayer support base. Just as mountain climbers who attempt to scale Mount Everest establish a base camp for communication, parents of prodigals must choose wisely those who will keep them connected to the Lord as they climb the treacherous slopes of intercession. Whether you reach the summit or not, your prayer team is vital.

⟢⟢⟢

What kinds of prayers make a difference? Prayers rooted in faith and obedience that have been affirmed by other mature believers and offered with dauntless persistence make a difference. Prayers that make a difference result in an amazing transformation in the one praying. And prayers that emit an unmistakable, inviting homing signal for our prodigals can save their lives.

At the end of each of the following chapters you will find a *Prayer Starter.* These ideas are meant to encourage you to go deeper into your prayer life through visualization and contemplation. Take your time when using these suggestions. They require an attitude of quietness. Likewise, a set of *Prayer Strategies* will give you a way to check how you're doing in using the five types of prayer we found most helpful. Challenge yourself to grow spiritually by making time for these exercises. You'll be glad you did.

Part Two

COPING

Chapter 4

USING PRAYER TO COPE WITH THE PAIN

GOD DOES NOT GIVE US OVERCOMING LIFE:
HE GIVES US LIFE AS WE OVERCOME.
—OSWALD CHAMBERS

Ever wish you could have someone else's life instead of yours? Of course. Most parents look around and notice the families who seem to have perfect children. Those are the families we envy. Those "perfect children" aren't always so perfect upon closer inspection, but we compare anyway. And when your child is in trouble, the comparison really hurts.

A prodigal son or daughter stirs up so many awful feelings that some days are intolerable emotionally. Guilt and shame rob you of your self-confidence. Fear and dread rob you of your sleep. Anger robs you of your peace of mind. Grief robs you of your hope. How are you to cope with such an emotional barrage?

Prayer. Prayer. Prayer. You may have thought of prayer as something you do in church with a pastor leading, or you may have thought of prayer as something you do for someone else. Now you are about to expand the edges of your prayer life to fit around every need—including the need to cope with the complexities of parenting a prodigal. We are going to challenge you to be creative and communal in your prayers. Prayer is your best weapon to fight against all the forces that would destroy your child's spirit.

Be HONEST

This prodigal child thing hurts. Tell the truth to yourself and your friends. Stop trying to hide the pain. Don't be a martyr and suffer alone. When your child begins to stray from the hopes and dreams you had for her, face the fact that she is changing everything in your world too, whether she knows it or not. You and your loved ones are being forced to deal with issues that you never imagined you would face. How could your daughter wreak such havoc? How could your son make such poor decisions? Why haven't all the good things you've done as a parent worked?

The unanswerable questions are the beginning of the pain. You go over and over the same thoughts, wishing you could understand what is happening. Nothing makes sense. You're left with confusion and frustration that inhabit every moment no matter where you are or what you're doing. You feel yourself shrinking inside, becoming less of the person you used to think you were. Doubt floods the shores of your identity and you grope for new boundaries to define yourself and your family. None of these mental routines works. The only thing that works is to surrender your pain to the Lord.

Prayer Is POWERFUL: CAROL'S *Story*

Carol's mother lay on her deathbed. At fifty-one years of age a brain aneurysm struck, and she was hanging on by a thread. As Carol and her sister gathered the family outside the hospital room, one of their mother's dear friends arrived. She asked if she might be allowed to go into their mother's room and pray for her. Strict orders were posted to keep all visitors out, but Carol convinced the nurses to make an exception. Carol had grown up in the church but never knew anyone who prayed like this friend. Thirty minutes passed as they waited outside the door. Concerned about her mother, Carol entered the room. Mary, the friend, was on her knees on the cold, hard, terrazzo floor. Carol was shocked to think that she could have been kneeling there for such a long time.

Eventually Mary came out of the hospital room, saying, "Your mother will be just fine." Carol and her sister didn't know how to take Mary's optimism. The doctors certainly weren't offering that kind of hope. The aneurysm was inoperable and seeping. They gave her mother a slim chance of making it through the night.

Carol had to return home that night because she was separated from her husband and struggling to support her young children. Her business was their only livelihood. She left not knowing whether she would ever see her mother alive again. As she drove the sixty miles to her home, she kept replaying the picture of Mary, on her knees, praying for her mother. She could not erase the image. After rushing her girls to school, Carol opened her shop with thirty minutes to spare. The stillness was penetrating. She pondered whether God could answer other needs in her life. Her marriage was over and she was scared.

A still, small voice inside said, "Pray like Mary did." Just then the phone startled her. Her sister was ecstatic, calling to report that their mother had come out of the coma and the doctors had found a procedure to stop the bleeding. Mary had been right! Carol hung up the phone sobbing.

She knew that if God listened to Mary's prayer, then He would hear hers too. She started talking to God even though she didn't know how. She admitted to Him that she couldn't do anything else on her own. She begged Him to help her, to please show her what she had to do about her failed marriage. All of a sudden, a deep, indescribable peace washed over her entire being. God was telling her to let Him handle everything. He did what He said He would. The decisions she needed to make became clear, right down to the details of what to do with her business and her marriage. Mary's faith and prayer life opened a whole new source of power for Carol, which would become valuable years later when one of her daughters became a prodigal. Carol learned to present her needs before the King and let Him handle the rest.

In Carol's case God appeared to be using the experience to strengthen her faith and prepare her for future trials. Of course, not every prayer is answered in the same way that Carol witnessed. Sometimes God says, "Not your will but Mine." The important thing to remember is that He will answer your prayers.

NAME *That* PAIN

In the next four chapters we will describe four types of pain that parents of prodigals experience, but there are many variations of these. No matter what label you give the pain, being able to name it will help you know what to do. I (Brendan) have found in my psychotherapy work with people in pain that relief and direction come more easily if you can put your experience into words. When parenting a prodigal, there are times when you simply can't find the words. At those times, slow down and ask the Lord to give you the correct words to express what you feel.

As you read the chapters on guilt and shame, fear, anger, and loss, we trust you will start to recognize your own emotions. Take notes in the margin of this book or in your journal whenever you become aware of some hurt or painful part of being a parent to this child who refuses God's will. Remember to ask God to enlighten you about that when you talk to Him.

Being able to name or label an experience gives you a better sense of control than just being bothered by something that you can't identify. You may not know all the reasons for your feelings, but at least you know what you feel. Most of the time anger is a secondary feeling that kicks in to protect you from hurt or fear. If you feel angry, don't be afraid to feel it. But ask yourself what is the primary feeling underlying your anger. The main feeling groups are *mad, sad, glad,* and *scared.* If you can't come up with sophisticated names for your feelings, just figure out which of those four fits best.

Develop COPING Strategies

You have many coping techniques, some better than others. But everyone can benefit from enlarging his or her list of strategies. As you read the next four chapters, look for the techniques that might work for you. Jot them down and elaborate on the idea. Think of ways to apply the idea to your situation. Every strategy is a tool.

Picture a big toolbox in the trunk of your car, filled with a wide selection of tools, both exotic and ordinary. If you ran into car trouble, wouldn't you want plenty of tools at your disposal to get your car going again? You might need a flare or a crowbar or a fuse. Or maybe a flashlight would be exactly what you needed when there wasn't enough light to make repairs. God wants to expand your spiritual and emotional toolbox so you won't have to worry when trouble comes your way. In other words, be as prepared as you can be.

While vacationing at Lake McQueeney near San Antonio, I (DeEtte) sat on the water's edge enjoying the early evening's breeze. An unlikely pair of boys sat on the pier watching their cork bobbers, which they had baited with leftover french fries. One boy was thin and wiry with a bowl haircut. The other was oversized with a burr. They made no sound, intent on a successful catch.

Suddenly, as the smaller boy jerked his pole I saw the head of a three-foot-long catfish. With wide eyes he yelled at his buddy in a shaking voice, "Go get a net. Hurry! Run like the wind! Run like the wind!" Immediately the other boy scrambled to his feet and raced up the bank. Huffing and puffing, he returned with a net the size of a fish tank scoop, the kind used to scoop up guppies. Undeterred, the pint-sized angler dragged the net through the water attempting to capture his prize. Of course, the catfish got away and the net ended up at the bottom of the lake.

I thought of all the times I had attempted to rescue my children with tools and skills that were totally inadequate. My faith was the size of a guppy net. Although I had access to the Master Fisherman and His supplies, I wanted to use my own net. Ultimately my efforts failed. I was no match for the lure that seduced my children. It has taken a long time for me to learn new ways of coping and more effective ways of dealing with disappointment and discouragement. Even now, I have to be on guard against the tendency to return to the unproductive, futile efforts that failed in the past. Now I reach for the Master's net.

Pride can really get in the way when you need to learn something new. Decide right now whether you're going to hold tight to your pride or learn whatever new skills you need. If you need to learn how to confront your prodigal in love, ask for the courage to speak up with appropriately penetrating words. Maybe you need to learn when to be silent. Ask God to guard your lips and show you the cues for those times. Wisdom is knowing when you don't know the answer and being willing to ask.

PRACTICE, *Practice*, PRACTICE

The apostle Paul wrote these words of encouragement in one of his New Testament letters: "So don't get tired of doing what is good. Don't get discouraged and give up, for we will reap a harvest of blessing at the appropriate time" (Galatians 6:9).

I (Brendan) have found that I need to recharge my "spiritual batteries" every few weeks by listening to a tape on prayer or consciously observing Christian friends' prayer styles, looking for new ideas. One of my praying friends used to talk about how she prayed the same prayer in different ways—in a whisper, in writing, in the morning, in the afternoon—or even from a different perspective. She taught me to expand my approach. When my daughter Natalie was in college I prayed constantly for the Lord to bring Christian friends into her life. Friends were everything to Natalie. To my knowledge, the friends I requested never showed up. If they did, Natalie must have ignored them. Finally, one day I realized that I should pray for Natalie to seek new friends who loved Jesus rather than friends coming to her. A simple shift in the focus of my prayer helped me release my frustration with Natalie and with God.

Your natural reactions to hurt or fear won't change unless you consciously decide what to change and how to change it, and you actually work at doing it differently. Paul told us that we are a new creation in Christ, and we are. However, we still battle against our old sin nature that pulls us in the direction of dysfunction. Practice going to God *first* if you want to function well during this time of disappointment and discouragement. Let Him show you the areas in your own life that need to grow. Then you will be able to become a powerful intercessor for your child.

COPE

Here's an acronym to remind you what to do when you need to cope.

Calm down.

> Take a deep breath and talk yourself down from the ledge of despair. You will think better in a calm state than in a state of panic. If you can't accomplish that, call a friend who has a calming voice.

Obey God's commandments.

Don't sin just because you're upset. Take time to think about what you are saying or doing in response to your prodigal's behavior. Make sure you are in line with God's commands.

Prepare for the worst.

Of course you hope that the worst won't happen, but if you have thought about what you will do in the worst-case scenario, you'll be better equipped to handle whatever may happen.

Encourage yourself.

You need to hear encouraging messages that give hope. Stick with people who offer hope. If no one else in your immediate circle is offering this kind of support, then write affirming, reassuring messages on index cards and put them in your car, on the refrigerator, and on the bathroom mirror to remind you that God will get you through this.

PRAYER *Starter*

Think of a word picture for the pain you feel right now. Is this experience like an elephant sitting on your chest, or like walking through a fog, or maybe like trying to speak a foreign language? When a word picture comes to mind, write it down, say it out loud, then ask the Lord to change one of the elements in the picture. Notice which element He changes.

PRAYER STRATEGIES

Surrendered heart: Admit to the Wonderful Counselor that you are hurting or scared.

Faith-builder: Tell the Lord that you trust Him to walk with you through everything that happens.

Persistent prayer: Pray every morning for two weeks, asking God for new ways to cope.

Written prayer: Make a coping strategies list. List twenty things you can do to cope with your emotions. Include things to distract you, relax you, or comfort you. Place your hand on the list and ask God to bless you when you use it. Keep the list handy and use it when you feel overwhelmed by your emotions.

Shared prayer: Join or create a support group to encourage each other through Bible study and prayer.

Chapter 5

RELEASING GUILT AND SHAME

SAVE ME, O GOD,

FOR THE WATERS HAVE COME UP TO MY NECK.

—PSALM 69:1, NIV

Gloria and Jim watched the faces in their home Bible study group as they shared the events of the previous night. Their nineteen-year-old son, Brian, had attempted to hang himself in his closet after his girlfriend broke up with him. If Jim hadn't walked into Brian's room to borrow a computer disk, they would be making funeral plans. Brian was a moody kid, and Karli had been his first real love. In fact, Brian seemed to have made her his god, basing every decision on what Karli thought, regardless of his own values. Brian had quit attending church with the family because he and Karli stayed out late on Saturday nights. They were too tired to go.

When Jim found Brian turning blue from asphyxiation he grabbed his legs to take the weight off his neck and screamed for Gloria. Gloria frantically searched for scissors to cut loose the rope, then called 911. Paramedics revived Brian and rushed him to the hospital. After they stabilized him, the questions began. Police asked

51

why this healthy young man would want to die. Gloria and Jim felt responsible. They should have listened when Brian said that he and Karli were breaking up. They should have been more approachable. Instead, their son nearly died while they were in the house.

They expected their group to offer support and compassion. Instead, everyone sat in stunned silence. No one seemed to know what to do. Finally, one of the men in the group said, "Why did he do *that?*" The rest of the group stared at the floor and squirmed in their seats. Gloria and Jim's hearts sank. *Could these people who claim to know Christ have so little compassion?* None of the members of the group had ever known anyone who had attempted suicide, and they totally missed the importance of giving comfort and encouragement to a family shattered by such a frightening experience. Gloria and Jim left the meeting that night feeling more alone and ashamed than ever.

Avoid SHAME-INDUCING *People*

All too often Christian friends have no idea what it's like to have a child act destructively, perhaps even self-destructively. Misguided advice, awkward silence, or judgment is deadly at a time when hope and encouragement are desperately needed. Reactions like that shut you down. People who don't "get it" aren't emotionally safe enough for you to tell them the whole story or admit your inadequacies. Without that kind of safety, you don't know what to do with the shame. So, you struggle to carry it or to hide it. Either option is unhealthy.

To move beyond the guilt and shame you must recognize *toxic people*. Toxic people are those whose actions push you further into despair, who, no matter how well-meaning, lack empathy or stand in judgment. As Proverbs 25:20 says, "Singing light songs to the heavyhearted is like pouring salt in their wounds" (MSG).

The first thing that parents of a prodigal need is their friends' love. Then they need a place to sort out the facts about the situation.

Finally, they need the support of Christians who have access to God's ear. Christians who come boldly before the throne and intercede for a family in pain are fulfilling the command of Jesus to love one another and bear each other's burdens. Someone in Gloria and Jim's small group might have provided mentorship for Brian if he were willing to accept it.

Norm Wright says people typically fall into one of three categories when it comes to responding to parents in pain:

1. Those unable to handle the situation
2. Those who feel compelled to offer unsolicited advice
3. Those who overwhelm you with help[1]

You cannot avoid encountering such individuals, but you can remind yourself that you deserve genuine support.

IDENTIFY *the* GUILT *or* SHAME

Guilt and shame hide behind anger and fear like a rattlesnake in the bushes, just waiting to strike at your confidence. If you would ordinarily approach life with faith and hope, guilt or shame will introduce doubt to shake you off that foundation. You will find yourself looking for someone to blame. Depending on your personality, you may blame another person, yourself, or even God. Blaming keeps you in a state of agitation and robs you of peace.

When Vanessa and Natalie pursued partying or destructive relationships, I (Brendan) used to waste a lot of emotional energy railing about their choice of friends. Internally I would have a dialogue with myself that went something like this: *What a failure you are! If you had been a better mother they would make better choices. Why didn't you pay more attention? You're so self-centered!* The diatribe would go on and on until I wanted to crawl in a hole and die. Blaming their friends or myself was counterproductive. It took my energy away from renewal and hope.

Let go of the desire to blame. Begin focusing on what part of the guilt or shame is a signal for change and what part is simply anxiety or worry. You see, Jesus was absolutely right when He told His disciples that worry would not add one hour to their lives (see Matthew 6:27). It won't add an hour to your child's life either. Worry only redirects your emotional energy away from God and weakens your spirit.

FREE *from* SECRETS: BEVERLY'S *Story*

Beverly's thirty-seven-year-old daughter, Kathryn, had "hit bottom" close to ten times since the age of seventeen. Of course, what Beverly thought were *Kathryn's* bottoms were really her own. Beverly's role was rescuer. Each time Kathryn was in a new scrape — failing school, wrecking the car, going on drinking binges — Beverly couldn't imagine how it could be happening. She blamed herself for everything Kathryn did. She was guilty on every count. When she couldn't change Kathryn by praying every morning at 6, she started at 5, and then at 4. "Tough love" wasn't in her vocabulary.

In front of most of her friends Beverly put on a smiling face, acting as if her family were fine, in spite of Kathryn's struggles and her husband's drinking problem. She was busy helping others: volunteering at church and in the community, attending Bible studies. She loved cooking three meals daily and keeping a clean "happy" house full of animals, flowers, and kids. Beverly's horror stayed inside.

Fortunately she also had a safe group of friends, and she unloaded on a daily basis. They listened when she phoned, and they met together weekly. This child was killing Beverly from the inside out. Every time she was sure she couldn't take it anymore, another incident would stretch her limits a bit further.

But her limits truly were stretched to the breaking point when Kathryn was raped at knifepoint. Shortly thereafter, Beverly found herself standing on the eighth-floor balcony of a fancy hotel, staring into the lobby below and intending to jump. Suicide seemed easier than living with so much unhappiness. Fortunately, God intervened and used close friends to talk her into going to counseling. Of course, admitting that she needed a counselor was shameful too. If she were a Christian, shouldn't she be able to resolve these problems through Bible study and prayer? Shouldn't God be all she needed? Her husband was another obstacle. He certainly wasn't comfortable with telling a psychologist the truth about their family. He was miserable as well, but chose to ignore the problems.

As Beverly began to see things differently, her attitudes changed. She stopped feeling so responsible for the actions of other people. She realized that her family's dysfunction had contributed to Kathryn's problems. She wanted to stop faking and start learning a new way to live. Though her daughter's fractured lifestyle wouldn't totally heal for a number of years, Beverly's own coping strategies became healthier.

Looking back, Beverly wishes she hadn't kept so many secrets. She wishes their family could have talked more freely about their problems. She wishes she could have shown Kathryn how to deal with her feelings at an early age instead of hiding them. But she thanks God that they have learned to release their shame and accept God's love.

Secrets block the light. Secrets bind the secret-keeper in a tangled web of lies and deceit. Secrets indicate that we are living in fear and shame instead of trusting God.

Facing shame requires all of our strength. No one likes to see himself as a failure or to feel responsible for another person's actions when the outcome is bad. In his book *Parents in Pain*, John White writes:

The problems include your feelings—your hurt, your rage, your panic, your disappointment, your shame, your humiliation, your alternate wish to yell at someone (your spouse, your child, your child's friends, the schoolteacher) and to lock yourself in

the bathroom and talk to nobody. Look at them all. They
exist. They are part of the problem you face. Even the sense of
despair. And to look at them, to be able to face them fully and
honestly, and to size them up is the first step in solving them.
You cannot solve problems you close your eyes to.[2]

White captures the impact of so many feelings hitting a parent all at
once. You may feel like you are all over the map with your reactions.
For that reason, you must spend time praying and reflecting on those
feelings in order to find your way through them. James 1:5-8 says:

> If you don't know what you're doing, pray to the Father. He
> loves to help. You'll get his help, and won't be condescended
> to when you ask for it. Ask boldly, believingly, without a sec-
> ond thought. People who "worry their prayers" are like wind-
> whipped waves. Don't think you're going to get anything
> from the Master that way, adrift at sea, keeping all your
> options open. (MSG)

Close the options of shame and blame unless they direct you toward
necessary change in your attitude or action. When your anger or fear
points to underlying guilt feelings or shame, pay attention. Check
the rationality of your inner thoughts with someone you trust to tell
you the truth. Ask God to give you wisdom regarding the feelings
that haunt you. If you can't figure it out, see a trained counselor.
Finally, correct what needs correcting and release what needs releasing. Let your feelings function as signals, not as the controller of
your life.

PRAY *for* DISCERNMENT

Guilt and shame are not always appropriate responses for a parent.
Sometimes the prodigal is totally at fault for his choices. Ask the

Lord to help you discern who is responsible for the problems that led up to the prodigal's decision to abandon her faith. If you really don't find evidence that you erred, then let go of unnecessary guilt.

Mike McPherson's book *Parenting the Wild Child* points out, "[Satan] has one goal in mind: to steal your child by lying to him about his life's purpose and true source of happiness."[3] Those lies come from every direction, both subtle and blatant. Lies about sex, money, and God spew forth from rock stars, movie stars, and advertising gurus. None of us is immune to the steady, unavoidable diet of lies about what it takes to be happy—and certainly not our children. Rather than beating ourselves up with neurotic guilt or shaming ourselves unmercifully for our inadequacies, we should be on our knees pleading with the Creator to help our sons and daughters to see the truth and to give them the courage to act accordingly.

The PAIN of INADEQUACY: JOHN'S *Story*

John was the kind of dad who could fix anything. He always knew what to do. When his twenty-two-year-old son, Greg, was arrested for selling drugs at a rave party, John rushed down to the police station and quickly posted bail.

"What the heck were you thinking?" John demanded. Greg stared out the car window. "We told you not to take those disc jockey jobs. Rave parties are nothing but trouble. You know that!" Greg stared out the window.

Four months later John answered the phone.

"Uh, Dad, I'm in jail."

"What? How did that happen? You're on deferred adjudication. What are you talking about?"

"Well, I didn't do what I was supposed to do and they arrested me this morning. Dad, can you just come down here and get me out?"

After the second jail ordeal, John and his wife, Nancy, discovered that Greg had failed to fulfill his community service and to report for drug screens as ordered by the judge. In fact, he had lied to his parents about attending college, having dropped out of school the third week of the semester. Greg had been pretending to leave for school every morning, perpetuating the lie for four months. No one had known the truth, except Greg.

When the truth surfaced, John lost all confidence that he could "fix" this problem. He was scared for Greg, scared for their family, and scared that he had failed as a father. His life was spinning out of control.

Legal fees, bail bond, and court-ordered counseling drained the family finances. John worked longer and longer hours, partly to make more money and partly to distract himself from the emotional strain at home. He and Nancy rarely talked about the fear that their lives might be ruined, that they might never be happy again. They just pushed on, doing whatever had to be done. John became more and more irritable and tired. The least little provocation from a driver ahead of him on the freeway or someone too slow in the drive-thru line at the burger joint set off an eruption of anger and impatience. The pressure and worry mounted until migraines hit John like a sledgehammer. Missing work made him even more worried, but he couldn't control the migraines any more than he could control Greg.

When he talked with his pastor, John heard himself say, "I don't know what to do, and I hate that. I should be able to do something about this. I should have seen it coming. How could I miss that he wasn't going to school for four months?" The pastor asked John whether he trusted God to handle these problems.

"I can't expect God to clean up my mess."

"*Your* mess?" the pastor wondered.

"Yes. I failed as a parent and God is punishing me for it."

"What do you experience when you think about that?"

"I feel alone and overwhelmed. I'm afraid I can't solve this. I stay awake all night trying to analyze what happened, and I just get more tense."

The pastor reached across the table, touched John's arm, and said, "John, the Lord wants you to trust Him. He doesn't expect you to solve Greg's problems. He will use this awful time to work on Greg. Christ is in that jail cell. Christ is walking alongside Greg right now. Let Him fix it in the way that He knows is best. You see, His love is perfect. And so is His timing. Trust Him. You don't have to do this alone."

John couldn't speak. As the tension eased slightly, he realized that God is a God of peace. When doubts tried to creep back in, John remembered his pastor's words: "You don't have to do this alone." In order to reinforce this truth and remind himself to trust God, John began a nightly ritual of mentally laying down his fears and inadequacies before falling asleep. He pictured Christ standing by the bed saying, "Let me carry that for you tonight. I can handle it." And then John imagined giving the day's worries to Jesus and thanking Him for being there when he needed Him.

Parents like John need to accept that they have limits to their strength and abilities. The apostle Paul challenged us to realize that God's "power works best in weakness" (2 Corinthians 12:9). It's foolish to keep trying to solve all the problems yourself. God wants to use more than your intellect or cleverness. Instead of believing that the conflict is about your worth as a parent, let God heal your pain and free you to discover what He can do.

TOXIC *or* HEALTHY?

We suggest that you run a personal gut-check on your feelings and even ask a trusted friend for feedback. If you discover that your feelings are excessive or are not justified by the facts, then the shame or guilt is toxic. Toxic shame is the kind that leaves you believing that you are hopelessly defective and undeserving of acceptance. Healthy shame serves the purpose of self-correction and character growth. You realize that you are doing something wrong or embarrassing that is inconsistent with the person you want to be. Admit it and work toward changing in that area of your life.

God is the great shame-eraser. He does not want you to walk around burdened by shame and guilt. If He did, He would never have sent Jesus to pay for your sins. He wants you to deal with it and let it improve your integrity and ability to feel compassion for others as well as yourself.

Let God reveal to you whether your feelings are toxic. If they are, ask Him to remove the poisonous effects and release you to live honestly and humbly without the burden of unnecessary shame.

PRAYER *Starter*

Name the things that embarrass or leave you ashamed of yourself or your prodigal. Imagine that they are like a heavy, dark veil draped over your head, blocking the light. Ask God to remove the veil and bring you into the light of His love. Then tell Him what realistic, hopeful belief you want Him to give you in exchange for the guilt and shame. Remind yourself to think this new way on a daily basis.

PRAYER STRATEGIES

Surrendered heart: Tell Him how much it hurts and ask Him to hold you.

Faith-builder: As you affirm the new belief about your child or yourself, praise God for healing you of a toxic condition.

Persistent prayer: Guilt and shame sometimes take more than one "washing" to get rid of the stains. Instead of expecting miraculous change overnight, keep bringing your request for cleansing and purifying to the Lord.

Written prayer: Write all the adjectives you would like to be able to use to describe your child or yourself when this prodigal experience is behind you. Let God know that you believe it is possible with His help.

Shared prayer: Reduce shame by being willing to tell another person your secret fear about yourself or your child. Pray first and ask God to prepare that friend's heart to hear you with compassion and wisdom.

Chapter 6

CONQUERING FEAR

IT IS ONLY AS WE HAVE BEEN THROUGH THE DARKNESS WITH HIM THAT
WHAT WE KNOW WITH OUR HEADS SLIDES DOWN INTO OUR HEARTS, AND
OUR HEARTS NO LONGER DEMAND ANSWERS.
—VERDELL DAVIS

Satan's best weapon is fear. He whispers lies into your ear:

"Your son hates you."

"You've failed as a parent."

"Nothing you do will ever bring her back."

"It's all your fault. Give up."

"God doesn't care. If He did He wouldn't let something like this happen, would He?"

"You'll never see your daughter again."

Fear strikes like a terrorist, sneaking around in disguise, looking for ways to catch you off guard, and taunting you with its destructive power. Sometimes you don't realize how scared you are until your body absorbs all it can take and then screams at you for attention. Your head is pounding; acid erodes the lining of your stomach. You feel overwhelmed and incapable of coping. What can you do?

Fear can be conquered only by faith, and faith thrives on truth. So what is truth? You don't know what will happen to your son or daughter or whether he or she will ever return safely. There are no guarantees. What you do know is that God wants to help your child. You know that God hears your prayers. And according to Isaiah, God said:

> When you go through deep waters and great trouble, I will be
> with you. When you go through rivers of difficulty, you will
> not drown! When you walk through the fire of oppression,
> you will not be burned up; the flames will not consume you.
> (43:2)

That's truth. So tune out the lies and turn up the volume on the God channel. And be open to small signs that He is there.

The TRAIN WHISTLE: KAREN'S Story

As Karen stepped out into the cold morning air she heard it: the train whistle. The mournful sound pulled her thoughts back to another time of separation from Laurel (a time not so long ago when Laurel was a teenage runaway).

Her memories traveled back to the night when she lay in bed stiff with fear, listening to the train whistle drift up the Rio Grande River valley. Twelve-year-old Laurel had been gone for several days. It wasn't the first time she had run away, but the assault on Karen's mind was still the same. *Where is she? Is she sleeping in the back of a car or under a bridge? Does she want to come home, but can't? Oh God, is she dead?* Karen threw off her covers and crawled out of bed, trembling as she made her way down the hallway to Laurel's room. She went to her window and looked out at the cold, dark night. The train whistle blew again. She prayed, "God, I know You know where Laurel is. I know You can see her, even though I can't." Terrifying images of Laurel bound and gagged in a car or dead in a ditch haunted her mind. She shook her head to make them stop. Panic seized her and she wanted to scream, to run out into the night to find her daughter. Tears poured down her cheeks as her heart poured out her prayers: "Jesus, Your Word says You came down from heaven to do the will of the Father. You said the will of the Father is that You would lose none of those He has given You. Help me to have faith that You are protecting her. Please restore her to You and bring her home to me." Exhausted, Karen lay down on Laurel's bed. She clutched Laurel's pillow to her breast and buried her nose deep in its folds, trying to capture a hint of her daughter's smell. She fell asleep praying.

Several days later Laurel was found and brought home, only to disappear again, this time with the family car. Karen was terrified that Laurel would kill herself or someone else. Sick at heart, she called the police to file charges against her daughter. Within hours, the state police found Laurel and called Karen to come sign papers before they took her to juvenile detention. A friend drove Karen to the substation, and when she walked in Laurel gave her an icy glare. After signing all the paperwork, Karen put on her coat and walked to the door. Laurel ran after her.

"Mom, don't do this!" she screamed. "If you love me, you won't do this!"

Shaking, Karen opened the door and without looking back replied, "It's because I love you that I am doing this." Karen gently closed the door behind her, fumbled in her purse for her keys, and crunched through the ice-encrusted snow to her car. She started the engine and started to cry. She wondered what jail was like and if Laurel would be safe there. Male guards wouldn't abuse her, would they? What if she was beaten by older girls? Then God spoke to her heart: "Do not be afraid." Karen was extraordinarily aware of His presence, and a quiet peace settled over her. She remembered His promise from Hebrews: "Never will I leave you; never will I forsake you" (13:5, NIV). With renewed strength and courage, Karen knew she could continue to fight for her daughter's life.

The next morning she notified the family attorney about Laurel's incarceration. He assured her she was safe and promised to visit Laurel the next day. At noon the phone rang. Karen picked up the receiver and heard silence. She started to hang up, but something made her stop. A couple of seconds passed, then a recording asked if she would accept a collect call from, pause, "Laurel." Karen quickly pushed the pound key to accept the call and waited.

"Momma? It's Laurel." Her voice sounded timid and tired.

"How are you?" Karen asked.

"I'm OK. How are you?" Karen could hear harsh voices yelling in the background.

"I'm all right."

"Are you safe?"

"Yeah, it's not too bad. The food's pretty gross though." Silence.

"Momma? I'm so sorry." She started to sob. "I'm just so, so sorry."

"I know you are, sweetheart. I'm sorry, too. We're going to get help, I promise." Just then the recording came back on, informing them they had one more minute. Karen didn't want to waste a precious second.

"Laurel, do you know how much I love you?"

"Yes, Momma, I do. I love you, too."

At that moment, Karen heard a train whistle over the receiver. She knew the tracks ran right behind the juvenile justice center. She quickly asked, "Can you hear the train whistle, Laurel?"

"Yeah, I can!" she replied.

"Every time you hear the train whistle, honey, know I'm praying for you." Then the line went dead.

Laurel told everyone in the detention center that her mother was praying for her—and for them. God used those prayers to plant a seed of faith in her daughter's heart—and maybe others' hearts as well. Laurel is twenty-two now and living independently, beginning a career.

To this day, whenever Karen hears the distant whistle of a train, she prays for God to draw her children to Him and to help frightened children on the road find their way to their heavenly Father's heart and home. "With God all things are possible" (Matthew 19:26, NIV).[1]

The VALLEY of the SHADOW of DEATH

Depression and despair threaten to consume you as you try to make sense out of your prodigal's behavior. All the "what-ifs" start to contaminate your thinking until you can't sleep. Tossing and turning, just like Laurel's mom, you imagine the worst-case scenario: your child dead in a gutter or raped or lost forever. Or maybe he just never grows up.

In Psalm 23, David describes walking through "the valley of the shadow of death." David's description beautifully captures the essence of fear. There you are, walking through a dark valley, sensing the foreboding presence of evil as it casts a huge shadow over your path. The shadow seems so threatening. Yet, like Satan and his lies, most shadows are mere exaggerations of the actual object that casts the shadow. If you could only remember that, you could bring the fear back down to size and keep walking. If you could only remember that you are not camping out in the valley, but walking *through* it to a better place, you wouldn't be quite so timid. If you could only remember that the Lord God Almighty is at your side, you might even be fascinated by the experience. Think of it as an adventure. You might not know the extent of the valley or when you'd arrive on the other end, but you would know that God promised to be your guide and that He knows the terrain.

Let *Your* FEAR DRAW YOU CLOSER *to the* LORD

Prodigals cast an ominous shadow over their family's identity, leaving the family afraid that they will not recover. Whether fear manifests itself as worry or trying to control—both normal responses when something threatens your well-being—simply stop to realize that these are signals, calls-to-arms that direct you into a deeper reliance on God. If you allow fear to derail you, you will waste the energy needed for the journey.

LOVE *Casts Out* FEAR: SANDRA'S *Story*

Sandra hadn't heard from Julie in three weeks. The last exchange they'd had was in the kitchen when Julie came home to get her clothes. If only Sandra could relive that scene. The pale gray tone of Julie's skin and crumpled look of her clothes set Sandra off. "Look at you, Julie! Don't you care what you are doing to yourself?" Julie ignored her and went upstairs. Sandra followed her to her room.

"Mom, just leave me alone. I'm nineteen. I don't care whether I go to college. That's your dream—not mine."

"You're throwing your life down the toilet. For what? That bum you think you love? He just wants to use your car and get you to take care of him."

"Mom, stop! You don't understand. Ryan loves me." Throwing her clothes into a duffel bag, Julie ran down the stairs and out the door into the waiting car and sped away with Ryan. Sandra had no idea where they were going. What would happen to Julie? How many naïve mistakes would it take for her to realize what she had done?

One Tuesday afternoon Sandra sat on the bed in Julie's room and began to cry. "Oh Lord, I am so scared. What can I do? Where are You? Please take care of Julie." Trembling, Sandra didn't know what else to pray. She just knew her daughter needed help. Sandra knew that Julie wasn't ready to be a grown-up. Julie had frequently confided in her before she met Ryan. If only she had reached out to her the day she came to get her clothes. If only she could have said something to change her mind. If only she had told Julie how much she loved her.

Sandra fell to her knees. "Lord, would You let Julie know that I love her? Would You give her that message for me?"

Six months passed before Sandra heard from Julie. Winter ice had settled in the treetops outside the house when Julie pulled into the driveway. Sandra heard the crunch of tires on the snow and peered out the window. Her heart skipped a beat as she saw Julie emerge from the car. Racing out the kitchen door, she ran toward her broken daughter.

"Julie! Julie! I love you. I love you. I love you." Julie's body was thin and stiff as Sandra threw her arms around her weary child. "Come in and tell me how you are. I thought I'd never see you again."

"Mom, I missed you too. It's been awful! Will you forgive me?"

"Yes, yes, of course I will! I love you so much."

Julie couldn't tell her mother how low she had stooped because the shame was too heavy. She couldn't tell her how she'd lived with panhandlers and addicts, or how she ate only once a day, or how more than one guy had used her for sex and then laughed at her and called her stupid. Julie felt scared to come home until one Tuesday—while searching for money to buy food, she suddenly recalled her mother holding her as a young child. Thinking about her mother's love gave her the courage to leave. She didn't know why that memory came to her that Tuesday, but it changed her heart. Julie had no idea that her mother's prayer had passed through the gates of heaven and been dispatched in grace. Love had brought Julie home. Love, perfected by faith, casts out fear.

PRAYER *Starter*

Think about the fears that are haunting you. Imagine that they are mere shadows, not nearly as ominous as they seem. Ask God to guide you in your prayer time and to lead you through the valley. Ask Him to stay very close and to light your path.

PRAYER STRATEGIES

Surrendered heart: Are you trusting God with Your fears, or dwelling on them?

Faith-builder: Ask God for reassurance of His presence.

Persistent prayer: Are you spending more time praying than worrying?

Written prayer: Write a list of your fears today and date it. Two weeks from now, read the list again and notice what has changed since then. Read it again in six months.

Shared prayer: Jesus said that what two or more bind on earth would be bound in heaven (see Matthew 18:18-20). Find a prayer partner who has experienced the pain of worrying over a wayward child and ask her to pray that you will walk in faith, not fear.

Chapter 7

RECOGNIZING ANGER AND USING IT CONSTRUCTIVELY

A TROJAN HORSE SITS JUST OUTSIDE THE GATE OF
YOUR HEART. ITS NAME IS BITTERNESS.
—ANDY STANLEY

Most people don't like being faced with their own helplessness.
When prodigals flaunt their defiance or their destructive behaviors,
we feel hurt and scared. Unfortunately, those feelings may come out
as intense anger. Anger feels stronger, more powerful. You want to
do something to change the situation, but can't. And that makes
you mad.

Andrea was no exception. Painful memories preyed on her
mind, eating away at her hopes. She couldn't let them go—images
of her daughter, Tiffany, getting out of the car, her sleazy male
friend draped across the backseat in a drug-induced stupor. Tiffany
was smiling, pretending to be happy that she was wasting her life.
The lies about the job she'd lost and the money she'd stolen made
Andrea furious. Tiffany was living a lie.

Andrea's heart was filled with contempt for Tiffany, for her
druggie friend, for everyone who had ever messed up Tiffany's

life—herself included. She wanted to shake Tiffany, hard. Shake some sense into that impulsive chunk of her brain that turned good sense off like a bad fuse darkens a room.

This beautiful, broken daughter wasn't malicious. She was just off track and didn't seem to have a homing device to bring her back. Instead of searching for one, Tiffany pretended she wasn't lost. She pretended she was happy. She pretended she wasn't scared. She pretended God didn't love her. She pretended and pretended until she couldn't pretend anymore.

"How could she?" Andrea fumed. Andrea searched for understanding but found none because she had lived her life on the other side of the looking glass—always too responsible, thinking too much. She had been a "perfect child." At least that's what her mother had always said. She got her strokes for demonstrating good judgment. So why couldn't she impart that virtue to her daughter? How could this kid make these choices?

Screams welled up in her throat. Hurt and fear collided. Her jaw tightened, locking the anger down. She was going to explode. But what good would it do? Tiffany wasn't there. She had moved in with her boyfriend.

Andrea's husband, Greg, rolled over in bed and attempted a cuddle. The anger trapped inside detonated, and Andrea shoved his arm away. "Stop it! Leave me alone!" Greg didn't understand. He withdrew, rolled back to his side of the bed, and thought, *I won't try that again*. Lonely silence set in. Andrea and Greg felt a gulf between them at a time when they needed each other most.

ANGER *Is* NATURAL

Anger is natural and unavoidable. Andrea had reason to feel angry. Unfortunately, when one family member is angry the others feel it. Sometimes your anger toward the prodigal may be blocked because you don't have the opportunity to tell him how you feel. Or, worse, you know that whatever is said in anger will probably make things worse.

In its natural state, anger is constructive. Anger becomes destructive when it is not expressed appropriately and is packed down inside. In *The Applause of Heaven*, Max Lucado writes:

> Resentment is the cocaine of emotions. . . . It causes blood to pump and energy level to rise. It demands increasingly larger and more frequent doses. There is a danger point at which anger ceases to be an emotion and becomes a driving force . . . and like cocaine anger kills . . . physically, emotionally, and spiritually . . . it shrinks the soul.[1]

As with Andrea and Greg, sometimes one parent struggles with anger and the other doesn't seem to react at all. In a single-parent home, a single mom or dad suffers alone with no one to listen to her or his frustration. One needs to vent the anger in constructive ways before it turns into depression. Often women are taught that anger is not an acceptable emotion, while men are viewed as strong when they get mad. Men who tend to avoid conflict may be scared of their wives' anger or their own. In order to avoid the conflict, they go into an emotional shell, like a turtle during a hailstorm, hoping the storm will pass.

Couples must allow each other to experience different reactions to events in their prodigal's journey. Dialogue is the best way to honor your partner and to help your partner sort out his or her own feelings. Dialogue means listening, validating, and empathizing—not adding your two cents, not criticizing or discounting the other person. Here's how it works:

- *Listen without reacting.* Whenever either parent's emotional temperature rises, the other should invite the angry one to talk about the feelings. Rather than judging the feelings or telling the spouse to "get over it," a supportive partner will *mirror* the feelings expressed—in other words, repeat them aloud to capture the essence of what the other is saying.

- *Recognize the triggers for the anger.* For example: "Every time I see a homeless person on the street I imagine Tiffany ending up there." Just the sight of a homeless person becomes a trigger for strong emotions.
- *Validate whatever can be validated.* Validating another's feelings does not necessarily mean agreeing or approving. It simply means letting the one expressing the feelings know that he is not crazy, that his feelings are understandable given what's happened.
- *Empathize.* Tell the one expressing the feelings what you imagine she feels. One way to know that you have hit the bull's-eye when trying to empathize is to watch for an involuntary reaction in the speaker's body when you say what you think she feels. Often people will sigh or nod, as if to say, "Yes! Someone finally gets it."

In the case of Andrea, Greg might have helped her if he could have said, "You seem angry. Would you tell me about it?" Andrea might not have been able to talk about her feelings right away, but she would know that Greg cared. Keeping the anger from spreading and being displaced on other loved ones would help Andrea avoid isolation.

When *All* YOU KNOW *Is* ANGER

Growing up in my (DeEtte's) childhood home, there was only one acceptable feeling: anger. We were not allowed to be sad, glad, or scared. My mother's continuous, unrelenting anger frightened me, but I survived by learning to get angry too. I know what the speaker meant when he said, "What you live with, you learn. What you learn, you practice. What you practice, you become." I lived with anger. I practiced it and I became an angry person.

Anger gave me power. Anger was control. Everything I did was ruled by the delusion that I had to have power and control. My parenting style reflected that belief and my children suffered crippling wounds to their souls because of my rage. I know now that when they turned their backs on me they were running away from my anger.

When I became a Christian I was confronted with the necessity of releasing this destructive emotion. There was no room in my spirit for the holiness, serenity, and joy God promised. I was terrified by the thought of giving up my most powerful weapon. I was afraid I would disappear. Anger had been my identity.

I actually had to acquire a taste for peace. It was so foreign, so different. When I turned my life over to God, the change was dramatic. Our first Christmas as believers was so quiet, nice, and uneventful that I felt like something was missing; well, that something was chaos and uproar. I had no idea how to act. I had to learn a whole new range of emotions.

Today I am unashamedly addicted to serenity. I protect my serenity as I would a rare gem. Now I give myself permission to be scared, or sad, or to experience huge doses of joy. By God's grace I have become a person who is easier to be around. I still have times that the anger wells up, but it doesn't rule. My goal is to respond instead of to react. Now my daughters feel safe around me when I express my feelings or opinions. I am so grateful to Christ for His transforming work.

Buried ANGER

Anger doesn't always look like anger. Sometimes a parent feels so hurt that his feelings collapse in on him. He may be so afraid of losing control that he drinks more than usual or sleeps too much. Another parent may walk around looking controlled while her stomach is churning acid. A mother may be taking medication for ulcerative colitis, not realizing that her intestines are smarter than she thought. She is trying to go on with her life, even though her son has forsaken his relationship with the family in order to practice a gay lifestyle. Her head tells her that she accepts her son's choices, but underneath she is furious and ashamed, wondering, *Why did this happen to our family? Are we defective parents?* She doesn't accept her son's choices. She wants him to change. To blow up or disown him would be politically incorrect. So she buries the anger. She swallows the pain until her colon screams.

Blaming OTHERS

Another way we bury our anger is to displace it. Instead of recognizing how angry we are at our child, we find someone else to blame. Parents often insist that their young adult child see a Christian counselor. They want the counselor to fix their child. When the counseling fails, the parents may fall into blaming the counselor rather than remembering that their prodigal has a free will. The prodigal is well aware that the parents have an agenda for the outcome of counseling. For that reason, counseling is not likely to succeed until the young person independently seeks help.

I (Brendan) worked with a young man who had been sexually molested as a child by a male relative. Although the family sought counseling as soon as they knew about it, the damage had already been done. When the boy grew up he began to experiment with homosexuality. He was ashamed and knew that God did not want him to do it, but he kept getting deeper and deeper into the lifestyle. He even started using the drug Ecstasy to anesthetize himself so he could perform sexual acts. This young man said he wanted to change. He said he loved God and wanted to be a good Christian, but he wasn't willing to give up his friends or the drugs. He wasn't ready to change. No counselor could effect a change until he was willing. Yet his parents were angry with me.

FACE *the* FEELINGS

What can an angry parent do? Under the Holy Spirit's inspiration the apostle Paul wrote, "'Be angry, and do not sin': do not let the sun go down on your wrath, nor give place to the devil" (Ephesians 4:26-27, NKJV). God understands your anger. He, too, is angry that your child is rebelling. The enemy has thwarted His wonderful plans for your son or daughter. Rather than succumb to bitterness or rage, you must pray for wisdom in handling your anger and seek the counsel of wise friends. Here are five steps for effectively facing angry feelings. If you take these steps, your anger can be helpful. Yes, helpful. Anger can teach you about yourself.

EXPRESS THE FEELINGS

Make a list of everything you are angry about. Don't worry about whether the items listed are big or small, rational or irrational, valid or not valid. Just get them on paper. Read what you wrote and notice any connections. Decide whether you would benefit from telling someone what you are angry about.

Allow another person who cares to hear or witness your feelings. Keeping emotions bottled up inside is dangerous. Dr. Dean Ornish, author of *Love & Survival: 8 Pathways to Intimacy and Health* and a research cardiologist, has shown that people who isolate themselves emotionally are at a much greater risk of early death or serious illness.[2]

Ask a good friend or your spouse what he or she thinks would happen if you told your prodigal your feelings. Deciding when to confront the person triggering the anger is tricky. Sometimes it is important for your child to know how angry you feel. Other times, your child knows all too well, and expressing the anger to your prodigal could stimulate even more rebellion. Basically, the decision should be made through prayer and with consideration for what the effect will be. If release is the main goal, then get the anger out by writing, talking to a support person, or at least talking to yourself.

Find physical ways to release muscular tension. Aggressive activities like tennis, running, kickboxing, or tearing up old telephone books and stomping on them are excellent ways to vent. Passive activities like deep breathing, stretching, massage therapy, or quiet time reflections like those in appendix A are also effective. Remember that the body does not lie. It will hold all your feelings until you express them. The sooner you release your feelings, the lower the risk of health problems.

CONFESS INADEQUACY

The truth is, we are all inadequate. The Lord has pointed out this fact to us repeatedly in His Word, but we forget. We want to be good enough. Sometimes we aren't. When we aren't, we must learn to view these times as opportunities for accelerated growth.

Confession involves two attitude changes. First, we must see our inadequacy the way God sees it—not as proof that we are worthless, but proof that we need His help. Second, we must desire to change our behavior. Like the first three steps of the Alcoholics Anonymous twelve steps, we must admit that we are powerless over the choices of our children, confess that only God can help, and then surrender our anger to Him.

MAKE CHANGES

We cannot afford to repeat ineffective patterns. No matter how strongly our instincts prompt us to defend ourselves by verbally attacking, or avoiding and ignoring our anger, we must refuse to follow those instincts. They are futile.

Face the anger. Put it into words. Then generate options for managing the anger or for solving the problem. More than likely, the solutions you believed would solve the problem have not worked and are helping to perpetuate the rebellion and disconnection.

Remember the Serenity Prayer. Change the things you can and stop trying to change the things you cannot change. If your daughter refuses to seek God, quit lecturing her about going to church. Start treating her the way Jesus would. Think of the woman at the well. Jesus met her where she was. He let her know that He knew her flaws, but He didn't judge her. He noticed that she was at the well, seeking water. Then He described living water. In other words, He used the very thing she was pursuing to challenge her thinking and perspective. He didn't ask her why she wasn't practicing religious activities.

Change your approach. Get out of your comfort zone. If you are angry, admit it and understand it.

Don't let your anger destroy what is good in your life.

LEARN MORE EFFECTIVE RESPONSES

Recognize what your response pattern has been. If it hasn't been working, try other kinds of responses. Sometimes listening more and saying less is very surprising to the prodigal. Sometimes written communication works better than talking. Write a letter, have someone you trust read it to screen out anything that could be construed as manipulative, and then send it to your child.

Attend parenting seminars or meet with a counselor to get new ideas. Listen to tapes of sermons or talks on forgiveness or patience or any topic that seems relevant to your specific situation.

Do something different.

RELEASE RESENTMENT

Resentment freezes your heart. Releasing resentment frees your heart to love again.

Make a list of all your resentments, small or large.

Speak or write the reasons you are not ready to let them go and the reasons you are ready to let them go.

Observe your comments. Notice what is blocking you from releasing them.

Ask the Lord to free you from the obstacle. Imagine Christ telling you to place the resentments at His feet and to allow Him to take care of them.

PRAYER *Starter*

Peace is the opposite of anger or bitterness. Pray for the peace that transcends all human understanding and let it guard your heart and mind from becoming bitter. Read Philippians 4:7.

PRAYER STRATEGIES

Surrendered heart: After you acknowledged your anger, did you ask God what He wants you to do with it?

Faith-builder: Which way of dealing with your anger is better: God's or yours?

Persistent prayer: If the anger hasn't disappeared, keep praying for wisdom regarding the source of your feelings and the actions God desires.

Written prayer: Write three victories you had this week in dealing with anger. Praise God for His help.

Shared prayer: Ask a friend to pray for you as you deal with a specific aspect of the anger. Use the phone or e-mail if getting together in person is difficult.

Chapter 8

GRIEVING LOSSES

THE LORD GOD WILL WIPE AWAY TEARS FROM OFF ALL FACES.
—ISAIAH 25:8, KJV

No matter how many children you have, if one is lost you suffer intense grief. A woman we met at a writers' conference told us about her six children. Five of them were quite successful but one was an alcoholic who, in spite of his upbringing, swore he would never set foot in a church again. The eyes of that mother told a tale of sadness and longing. She hoped her son would choose life instead of death, but his future looked grim. She whispered to me that she prays daily for him even as she grieves her loss.

The Parable of the Prodigal Son, also called the Parable of the Lost Son, is actually the third in a sequence of parables Jesus told about lost things; the other two parables are about a lost sheep and a lost coin. Such repetition suggests not only that God cares when we are lost, but also that God wants us to learn from the losses in our lives. In those parables, Jesus kept saying, in essence, "My love is relentless." His sorrow for those who are lost is obvious, and He knows your sorrow too.

COUNT *the* LOSS

In his book *Finding My Way: Healing and Transformation Through Loss and Grief,* John M. Schneider writes that we must find our path through grief by asking three questions of ourselves:

1. What is lost?
2. What is left?
3. What is possible?[1]

If we consider what was lost when our child went astray, each of us may come up with different answers. Some have lost regular contact with their child. Others have lost hope that their child will ever know the splendor of the Lord's love and provision. Still others have lost significant amounts of money trying to help their prodigal with therapy, loans, car repairs, rent, or tuition. These losses changed the quality of their lives.

Whatever the loss, you must grieve it. Naming the losses helps you understand the pain better. In a manner similar to funerals, where the one who has died is named, remembered, and honored, you must validate the importance of what is lost. For some, merely telling a caring person is enough. But most of us need a ritual or a clear statement of the loss. One way to accomplish this is to write "Loss" at the top of a page and list all the losses you have felt as a result of your prodigal child's decisions. The losses may be small or monumental. You may be grieving the wedding you'll never attend or the grandchildren you'll never know or the family business that will never be passed on. Maybe you had always hoped that you and your child would become good friends as adults. After recording the losses, reflect on their impact. Honor the truth that living with the loss hurts. Then assess what is left.

When grief hits, you feel as if nothing good is left, or that what is left doesn't matter. But it does. Chances are that the older brother in Jesus' parable witnessed his parents' grief after his sibling left and felt cheated or discounted even before the prodigal returned. He probably wished that the parents would appreciate that he was left. He probably wanted his parents to become closer to him during that time. If they dwelled only on the son they had lost, then they really had lost two sons in the process. If one of your children strays, you must invest in the family remaining.

When we ask ourselves, "What's possible?" the focus shifts to a very important, basic decision about how to live with this prodigal experience. This is the point where we choose a strategy and where prayer is central.

Hagar, Abraham's servant who bore his first son, wept as she sat in the wilderness of Beersheba feeling the pain of her fractured life. She and her son could no longer enjoy acceptance among the family as they had known it. Hagar believed that her son would die, and she couldn't stand to watch it happen. How many mothers have thought those same thoughts? Genesis 21:16-20 tells us that God noticed her pain and sent an angel to reassure her. God honored the losses of Hagar and Ishmael, and He promised that they would live meaningful lives. God didn't restore them to Abraham's tent, but He helped them adjust to their new lives. They survived the loss.

KEEP *Your* FAITH

One of the saddest losses of the prodigal experience is when parents lose their faith in God. Many parents have operated on an assumption that if they do everything right, God won't allow bad things to happen to them or their children. This attitude is naïve and self-centered. If we believe that God is managing a broken world full of broken people who influence other broken people, then we have to accept that bad things can happen to good people. And good people can certainly do wrong things. The Ten Commandments were given to humble us with the piercing knowledge that we cannot measure up to God's standards, no matter how hard we try. We must rely on God's grace and mercy.

What if Ruth and Billy Graham had given up on God when their son Franklin was rebelling and defying everything they wanted him to become? Both their ministries would have crumbled in hypocrisy and their son might not have returned to the faith of his childhood. Instead, they relentlessly prayed for Franklin and loved him through all his prodigal years. They believed that God had a plan and they trusted Him.

LOST *and* FOUND: PAT'S *Story*

A therapist friend, Pat, related the story of her prodigal daughter's unwanted pregnancy. Her daughter, Kathleen, had suffered the consequences of impulsive behavior since adolescence. Drug experimentation, shoplifting, and bad choices for boyfriends were her modus operandi. In her early twenties Kathleen found herself pregnant following a one-night stand; she didn't even know the name of the baby's father. Though Kathleen chose adoption over abortion, Pat was overwhelmed with grief. She would never know her first grandchild. Her heart ached with the seriousness of the decision. She couldn't raise the child herself, but saying goodbye before she ever knew this baby was excruciating. All the ideals she'd had about being a grandmother sank in the mire of an unwanted pregnancy.

Three months into the pregnancy, Pat sat in a therapy session with a woman she'd counseled for several years. Just two years prior, the counselee's ten-year-old daughter had died suddenly from a viral infection during a family vacation. Having lost her only child, the woman and her husband worked through layers and layers of sadness and anger over those two years. Finally, they decided to try in-vitro fertilization because she had fertility problems and was in her forties. Several attempts failed and the couple talked of adoption, but they weren't eligible for a conventional adoption because of their ages. As Pat sat listening to the woman talk about how she felt her main purpose in life had been to be a mother and now she had lost that, Pat experienced an undeniable awareness that God was at work. His amazing ability to work all things together for good was unfolding in that very moment. Pat told the client about her daughter's intention to give her baby up for adoption and asked whether she and her husband might be interested in talking to Kathleen. Now, as a therapist, Pat knew there were all kinds of ethical dilemmas with suggesting that a patient adopt her own daughter's child. She had to transfer the couple to another therapist. But she was absolutely clear that God had brought these unrelated life tragedies into alignment.

The couple chose to adopt the baby. The adoptive mother and Pat were on either side of Kathleen as she birthed a beautiful, healthy baby boy, and the adoptive mother began nursing the baby in the hospital with the help of hormones and a lactation specialist. God provided a good home for Kathleen's baby and He healed a gaping wound in the lives of the couple who adopted the baby. Pat remembered the passage in 1 Samuel 1:27 in which Hannah said, "I prayed for this child, and the Lord has granted me what I asked of him" (NIV). The family who'd lost their daughter had prayed for another child and the Lord used Pat and her daughter's loss to answer their prayers.

PRESENT *the* LOSSES *to the* LORD

A natural tendency when people are grieving is to pull inside themselves, to clam up and shut down. Shutting down protects a person from being hurt again. The world doesn't feel emotionally safe. The problem is that one cannot selectively "shut down" some parts and leave others open. As a hurting parent shuts out people around her, she begins to shut God out too. This process can take the form of anti-dependence—that is, "I don't need your help!" It can also manifest as giving up and not caring.

Either way, you must use prayer to stay open to the Lord's help. Remember the words of the psalmist:

Praise the Lord, O my soul,
and forget not all his benefits—
who forgives all your sins
and heals all your diseases,
who redeems your life from the pit
and crowns you with love and compassion.
(Psalm 103:2-4, NIV)

You don't know *how* the Lord will redeem your life from the pit, but you must trust that He will. Like the little boy who offered the loaves and fish to the disciples without knowing how Jesus would use them, offer your circumstances to the Lord. He knows how to transform the worst of circumstances into miraculous healing.

PRAYER *Starters*

Find photos of your child at a younger age when you still believed that her life would go smoothly and be filled with joy. Spread out the pictures on a table. Do you remember how much you wanted for this child? Feel the sorrow and loss. Then quietly scoop up the photos and lift them as if you are giving them to another person. Ask the Lord to take the pain and disappointment from your heart and set you free to live in faith. Imagine Him taking those photos the way He took the loaves and fish. Trust Him to work a miracle in order to meet the needs of those you love.

Think of a symbol (like the train whistle in chapter 6) that closes the distance, no matter how far, and use it as a reminder to pray for your prodigal and those around her.

PRAYER STRATEGIES

Surrendered heart: Tell God how much you miss the way it used to be or the way you thought it would be. Ask Him to help you let go.

Faith-builder: Ask God to show you an example of how He can use your loss to minister to someone else in need.

Persistent prayer: Pray through the tears. Don't give up.

Written prayer: Write a "Dear God" letter and tell Him what the hardest part is for you. Ask Him to help you say goodbye to the shattered dreams.

Shared prayer: Tell a friend that you are grieving and ask for prayer support.

Part Three

ENTRUSTING

Chapter 9

PRAYING FOR PROTECTION

PRAYER IS NOT CONQUERING GOD'S RELUCTANCE,
BUT TAKING HOLD OF GOD'S WILLINGNESS.
— PHILLIPS BROOKS

You've overcome the grip of fear and shame but your child is still in harm's way. The world is conniving to win your child's heart and soul. No matter how profound God's Word is, it's hard to compete with the flash and instant gratification the world promises. Alcohol, drugs, sex, the Internet, false religions, and money offer a siren call to your child as he searches for significance. You may question whether prayer can counter such destructive forces. I (Brendan) like to remember Edward Everett Hale's advice: "I am only one, but I am one. I cannot do everything, but I can do something; and what I can do, that I ought to do; and what I ought to do, by the grace of God I shall do."

Imagine that your prayers are missiles aimed at intercepting the dangers that threaten your rebellious or prodigal child. Focus on the mighty power packed into each word when you enlist the will of God. Listen to the promise of Psalm 34:5-8:

Those who look to him for help will be radiant with joy;
no shadow of shame will darken their faces.

> I cried out to the Lord in my suffering, and he heard me.
> He set me free from all my fears.
> *For the angel of the Lord guards all who fear him,*
> *and he rescues them.*
> Taste and see that the Lord is good.
> Oh, the joys of those who trust in him! (emphasis added)

You cannot know exactly what God will do with your prayers. He may "nuke" the enemy and bring your child home quickly. He may not. Your part is to do what you can to activate His power and intervention.

LISTEN *When* GOD *Is* CALLING

In his book *Fresh Wind, Fresh Fire*, Jim Cymbala, pastor of the Brooklyn Tabernacle, shared the remarkable story of how his daughter Chrissy returned to Christ and to her family through the power of prayer. Jim and his wife, Carol, suffered an agonizing separation from Chrissy when she defiantly left home. Just as most parents who stand in leadership tend to do, they found themselves ministering to others when their own hearts were breaking. One Tuesday night during a church prayer meeting the Spirit of the Lord moved a woman in their congregation to send a note forward. The church member felt urged to intercede for Chrissy. Jim shared their situation and asked for prayer. He said those prayers sounded like labor pains when a woman delivers a child. Within thirty-two hours Chrissy came home, repented, and sought fellowship with her family and her God. Jim recalls his daughter's homecoming:

> "Daddy," she said with a start, "who was praying for me?
> Who was praying for me?" Her voice was like that of a
> cross-examining attorney.

"What do you mean, Chrissy?"

"On Tuesday night, Daddy—who was praying for me?"
I didn't say anything, so she continued:

"In the middle of the night, God woke me and showed
me I was heading toward this abyss. There was no bottom to
it—it scared me to death. I was so frightened. I realized how
hard I've been, how wrong, how rebellious. But at the same
time, it was like God wrapped his arms around me and held
me tight. He kept me from sliding any farther as he said, 'I
still love you.' Daddy, tell me the truth—who was praying for
me Tuesday night?"

I looked into her bloodshot eyes, and once again I recognized the daughter we had raised.[1]

What a strong reminder to pray. Not all prodigals will respond like
Chrissy, no matter how many people pray, because God always gives
the prodigal a choice. But if you don't intercede you may miss an
opportunity to alter events on your prodigal's journey. Trust God to
decide which events to change.

Be PERSISTENT

In an article titled "A Pattern for Persistence," Sandra Higley lists
six elements of persistence that she discovered in the Matthew
15:21-28 account of the Canaanite woman who persisted in her
request for Jesus to heal her daughter:
* Acknowledge who God is.
* Be specific about the need.
* Don't give up in the face of silence.
* Ignore the negative remarks of others.
* Be humble.
* Stand firm.[2]

Are any of these elements difficult for you? Do you have trouble figuring out what to pray? Make a list of the thoughts that plague you when you worry about your prodigal. Then pray specifically for the Lord to intervene in each one. Do friends or family criticize you for the way you are dealing with your child's problems? Ask the Lord to free you from the pressure and give you peace. Is your pride in the way? Are you angry with God? Submit all your feelings to Him and ask for His help. Do you feel weak or shaky when you are praying for your son or daughter? Ask the Lord to give you certainty of your beliefs and courage to stay the course.

Trust GOD to Use the BAD EXPERIENCES

Two days before my (Brendan's) daughter's best friend, Elizabeth, reached her eighteenth birthday, she died from alcohol poisoning. As the minister offered Elizabeth's eulogy, I studied the faces of dozens of stunned teenagers. The myth of invincibility shattered before their eyes as they stared at Elizabeth's cold, lifeless body in the casket. Death became an irreversible truth. My daughter Natalie grieved for years. Today, she remembers her friend by displaying a mirror that belonged to Elizabeth on the wall of her apartment. Natalie made life-changing decisions about her own life the day of Elizabeth's funeral.

When God is ready to move the heart of your child, He will use life events in amazing and unexpected ways. Your child's heart may be inaccessible to you but it is easily accessible to God. Even when your child seems to be avoiding God with all her might, pray for God to use every experience to open her eyes and guide her to make transforming decisions. James R. Lucas, author of *Proactive Parenting*, writes:

> You can't make a child be wise. Children's hearts must deal
> with or avoid God directly; the ultimate responsibility for this

is out of your hands. You aren't a mediator between God and your children because Christ already has that job. All you can do is make the choice for them as simple as possible.[3]

Remember that the Holy Spirit may be at work long before you sense a change and that something as simple as a word spoken at precisely the right time could awaken your child to the presence of God. Preaching at precisely the wrong time could dampen the spirit and cloud the opportunity for God to work in the heart of your son or daughter. The challenge for parents is to simplify our message and live it, to show our prodigal children the fruit of a life lived in tune with the Holy Spirit.

INTERCEDING

Although your prayers will focus on specific events or needs, like a runaway son or an appointment your daughter has with the abortion clinic, there are far more times when you don't know the specifics but you know you need to pray. Those are the "basic" protection prayers: "Lord, I don't know where Justin is tonight but I ask you to set your angels around him to guard his steps and to block the Enemy." Asking the Lord to use His power on behalf of your child takes mindful commitment.

That kind of commitment reminds me of a phenomenon of nature I (Brendan) discovered on a whale watch in Cape Cod Bay one summer. The naturalist pointed out two whales that appeared to be floating dead in the water side by side. She explained that the whales were logging, a term for the way whales sleep. Whales sleep in groups for twenty-minute intervals because they can allow only half of their brains to sleep at a time. Otherwise, they would forget to breathe, and drown. Instantly I made a connection with the prayer life of parents. When our children "forget to breathe"—that is, when they shut down all common sense and neglect the basics of their spiritual upbringing—we parents can intercede and function like the other half of their spiritual brains, preventing them from drowning in their rebellion. We can keep the Holy Spirit working actively in their lives.

In his book *Intercessory Prayer*, pastor and author Dutch Sheets writes, "We are like a magnifying glass in one sense—no, we don't add to or magnify God's power—but we do let the 'Son' shine forth through us, directing His light to desired situations, allowing it to 'strike the mark.'"[4]

The TRAP

In a way, your prayers set a trap for the forces of defeat that threaten your prodigal. Whether it's the loser boyfriend or the faulty beliefs about happiness, imagine that your prayers can ensnare the Enemy's wily tricks and stop them before they damage your child. In their book *Prayers That Prevail for Your Children*, Cliff Richards and Lloyd Hildebrand name *seven kinds of protection*. Parents of prodigals should focus their prayers on all seven of these areas:

1. Protection from temptation
2. Protection from evil
3. Protection from evildoers
4. Protection from negative influences
5. Protection from Satan
6. Protection from sin
7. Protection from wrong thinking[5]

Just reading the list made me (Brendan) shiver to realize how many ways our prodigals can be drawn into darkness. Satan cleverly sets traps that don't even look like traps at first. Discerning a trap from a harmless experience is difficult for a mature adult, much less for a young person who is optimistic and eager to taste all that life has to offer. We need to set a few traps of our own.

Recently, my husband, Dan, and I had a series of hair-pulling episodes with possums that managed to nest in the crawl space between the first and second floors of our house. Being nocturnal creatures, naturally they came to life just as Dan and I had fallen into a restful sleep. Their scaly tails would sweep and scrape across the plywood flooring directly above our bedroom. Then the screeching started, like the shower scene in *Psycho*. The *coup de grace* was when they banged their entire bodies against something stored in the attic — it sounded as if someone had hurled a refrigerator against the wall, tumbling its contents onto the floor. Needless to say, Dan and I would be sleepless for hours after one of these episodes. I lay there imagining a creature scratching through the ceiling and landing on my chest. I even took the scenario to the absurd, convincing myself of sudden death from the shock. And when Dan went about trapping the critter, I was certain that he would be bitten by a rabid possum and die. We survived the ordeal, but sleeping in that bed was never the same. The whole incident left me feeling vulnerable and frustrated.

The pain and vulnerability felt by parents whose child is at risk make for sleepless nights with anxious imaginings. Powerlessness in the face of disaster is painful, especially when the person you want to protect is your child. Are you really powerless over the dangers your child faces? To some extent, the answer is yes. But prayer changes that. You have the power to plead your child's case before a merciful God. And God definitely has the power to trap the forces of evil and cancel their schemes. With the psalmist, we can renew our confidence in Him:

> From the ends of the earth,
> I will cry to you for help,
> for my heart is overwhelmed.
> Lead me to the towering rock of safety,
> for you are my safe refuge,
> a fortress where my enemies cannot reach me.
> (Psalm 61:2-3)

Christ truly is a towering rock of safety, and you can count on that strength when you feel vulnerable and your heart is overwhelmed. You can also ask God to lead your son or daughter to the rock so he or she will be safe. And you can set a trap for the Devil by surrounding your child with prayers.

BELIEVE *in What* YOU CANNOT *See*

Like Noah building an ark for 120 years, not knowing how God would use it to protect all the animals and preserve life on this planet, you must keep building a haven of faith for your prodigal. Others may mock your efforts, but don't be discouraged. Pray hard. Pray until something happens. Noah had never seen rain, much less a great flood, but he kept on sawing that lumber and searching for those animals. He obeyed God's instruction even when it made no sense. You may not have ever seen a miracle, or your child may not have shown any evidence of wanting to change, but your prayers and your obedience to God's Word could bring it to reality.

In my clinical practice I (Brendan) have worked with a few long-term cases in which the clients overcame lifelong depression. During the years of working with these women there came several points in the process when despair was winning, no matter what I said or did. One day, in the midst of such a suicidal crisis, I heard myself say, "Lisa, you hang on to my faith until yours comes back." At first it sounded silly — pretty desperate, too. Then, as I contemplated those words and I saw the relief in Lisa's eyes and watched her whole body relax, I realized that those words had come from the Holy Spirit. They sounded strange to me, but God knew exactly what Lisa needed to hear in that moment and He used my lips to deliver the message. After that, Lisa occasionally asked, "Can I hang on to your faith right now? I don't feel strong enough on my own."

I was so impressed by the obvious impact of offering my faith when another person lacked faith that I started praying for my grown daughters in the same manner. I pray that God will substitute my faith when theirs is inadequate; that somehow my daughters will feel the solid rock of safety when they are starting to go under, and my faith will be the life preserver that keeps them above water until they find faith of their own.

You have no way of knowing what God will use to intercede on behalf of your child. Give Him everything you have; He'll know what to do with it. Believe that He is working a plan.

JUST *in* TIME

One summer I (Brendan) took my two youngest children to Canyon Lake in the Texas hill country for a short vacation. We decided to rent a large Wave Runner and cruise the lake. The day was a beautiful, sunny Monday—no crowds of boaters or drunken college students. Five minutes into the ride the engine died and could not be revived. We spent two hours drifting, wishing we'd brought sunscreen, water, and oars (none had been provided).

We made futile attempts to flag down another boat. They just couldn't see us. As our frustration increased I felt how difficult it was to sit powerlessly waiting for events to turn around. At last, my ten-year-old son, Devin, jumped into the water and tried to pull the boat. Within no time the current separated him from us, the distance growing alarmingly fast. I had to jump in and swim with a lifejacket on, against the current, to reach him and pull us both back. Meanwhile, seven-year-old Christine was alone on the Wave Runner drifting away from us. My heart pounded and my lungs felt like they would explode, but I swam as fast as I could. We made it. Once we were all back aboard I grabbed a tree stump sticking out of the water and held on to it to keep us from drifting even farther into a little swamp area where rescue would be more difficult. We hung on for another hour until the half-alert teenage boy who ran the bait shop eventually came for us.

As I reflected on the harrowing event, I realized how amazingly powerful a parent's protective instincts are. In ordinary circumstances, there was no way that I would have been willing or even able to make the swim that I made that day. But the thought of losing my son or daughter propelled me beyond my natural strength. The threats you face with your prodigal child are more disturbing, but the compelling urge is the same. Watching your prodigal drifting farther and farther away revs up all your survival instincts. Every neurochemical in your body rallies to the cause. That's probably why you can't sleep at night.

Your prayers to the all-powerful and loving God can stop the forces of evil just in time to rescue your child from Satan's devious schemes. You may find yourself "hanging on to a tree" as the currents of time work against you—but hang on.

Preacher and author Max Lucado once served as a missionary in Brazil. He writes:

> The Brazilians have a great phrase for this [steadfastness]. In Portuguese, a person who has the ability to hang in and not give up has *garra*. Garra means "claws." What imagery! A person with *garra* has claws which burrow into the side of the cliff and keep him from falling.[6]

Your prayers function like those claws; they burrow into the Rock of Ages and help you hang on. You have no guarantees that your child will be safe, but your prayers could be what helps your prodigal hang on and not give up.

PRAYER *Starter*

Choose one of the seven types of protection listed in this chapter and pray that the Lord would provide that for your son or daughter today. Imagine that your faith is shining a light into the darkness, sending a beacon of hope into the despair.

PRAYER STRATEGIES

Surrendered heart: Tell God that you want to protect your child but you cannot do it without His help. Ask Him to work His plan, not yours.

Faith-builder: Practice daily going to the Rock that's stronger than you. Feel how solid He is. Be aware of His presence.

Persistent prayer: Pray for the protection of your child every day. Don't miss a single day for two weeks.

Written prayer: Write an example of ways the Lord could protect your child in each of the seven areas we discussed.

Shared prayer: Ask seven friends to each take one of the concerns you wrote and pray for that one specifically this week.

Chapter 10

PLEADING FOR REPENTANCE

THE FOCUS OF WHAT GOD IS DOING IN YOUR LIFE
TAKES PLACE *IN* YOU, NOT *AROUND* YOU.
—ANDY STANLEY

"Dad, don't call me. I don't want to talk to you." Austin's words stabbed Scott in the heart; the rejection hurt deeper than any he'd ever known. Scott and Austin had been so close throughout Austin's childhood. Even after the divorce, Scott stayed actively involved. He moved a few blocks from Austin's mother so Austin could go between the two houses any time. Scott had been at every sports event to cheer for Austin, and they had shared laughs as well as victories. Austin became an increasingly heavy drinker throughout his high school years, numbing his true feelings. His friends saw him as tough and angry, although he maintained status in the popular crowd.

During Austin's senior year his baseball coach refused to recruit him for the team because of his attitude. Austin had been the star player and could not accept this rejection. He had big plans to go to college on a baseball scholarship—this just couldn't be happening. Scott thought that he could help by talking to the coach and straightening things out for Austin. So he called the coach without discussing the plan with Austin. When Austin heard what his father had done, he felt embarrassed and reacted by focusing his rage on his dad. "I will never forgive you for that!" Austin screamed at his father.

Austin held to his promise for four years. Scott was not allowed to share any of Austin's college experiences. Austin would not accept phone calls or visits from Scott or Scott's wife, Vicky, who had enjoyed a close relationship with Austin in the past. The wall he built was more formidable than a bank vault door. For Scott the pain was excruciating. He and Vicky met regularly with a small group of Christian friends who prayed with them for healing of this wound. They asked God to soften Austin's heart toward his father and to bring Austin to repentance for his stubborn defiance.

Shortly after Austin graduated from college, his mother was diagnosed with breast cancer and the entire family began rallying around her. Standing in the waiting room of the hospital one night as they waited for word from the surgeon who had removed his mother's breast, Austin looked at his father sitting across the room and realized that he had been wrong. He knew that he did not want to lose his father any more than he did his mother. Click, click, click—the heavy vault door inside his heart started unlocking. All the resentments and hurts so carefully stored began to dissolve. He didn't know exactly what to do but he knew he wanted to speak to his dad. Tears filled his eyes as he put one foot in front of the other to close the distance between them in the waiting room.

Scott glanced up from the magazine he'd been using to fill the silence and saw his son with tears in his eyes walking toward him. Four years of disconnection had almost made him forget what it was like to feel Austin's love. But he knew that something had happened inside Austin and that, at this very moment, all the prayers were being answered. Scott stood up so he would be there for Austin in this monumental moment of repentance. The two men, father and son, embraced, sobbing and saying to each other, "I'm so sorry. I'm so sorry. I love you."

Repentance happens in an instant, but it can take years for the timing to be right. Sometimes a child's defiance has to run its course. Sometimes a tragic event has to happen to reset the prodigal's priorities. Repentance requires admitting the sin of pride, and that may be the hardest thing of all to admit.

Letting GO

Let go of what? What does the prodigal have to surrender in order to receive restoration to full relationship with God? Self-reliance. Some young people need to give up the lie that their friends are all they need. Others have to let go of an addiction or a self-defeating behavior. Admitting "I was wrong" means releasing the reins and clinging to God as if your life depends on it. Because it does. It also means accepting that you can only control what you do right now, today. Someone once asked Will Rogers, "If you had only twenty-four hours to live, how would you spend them?" He replied, "One at a time." Recovery from failures is a lifetime proposition given to us in "lifetimes" called days. "We can never touch the future or return to the past. Today is a lifetime."[1] Pray for your prodigal to repent today. Pray that he will choose to seek God with all of his heart, that he will overcome the pride and the lies and cling to Jesus as he lets go of the reins.

Old INSTINCTS BLOCK *Change*

When my (Brendan's) youngest daughter, Chrissy, was six years old, she took horseback riding lessons. Her instructor placed a riding crop behind her back, between her elbows, to remind her to hold her shoulders back. This meant that Chrissy could barely reach the reins while maintaining such a correct posture. She had to use her legs to signal the horse when she wanted it to turn or stop. I watched Chrissy struggle against the reflexive instinct to slump forward and grab the reins in order to feel more control. Gradually she learned to release the obvious means of control and trust other methods, and her riding improved.

Like Chrissy and her horseback riding lessons, your prodigal will struggle with an urge to rely on old instincts. God may be drawing him to repentance by gradually removing the things in his life that he has counted on. Whether your prodigal "hits bottom" or simply has to reckon with consequences, God is there teaching her to trust and let Him be in control. Like Austin in the earlier story, your son or daughter may have to reach a painful awareness before he or she will let go of the defiance. Often, a lack of repentance is simply refusing to let go. Pray for your prodigal to let go of her pride and see her life as God does. Only then will the pain of what she has done convince her to change.

Vanessa (Brendan's daughter) was homeless, seeking refuge from the August heat by sitting in the public library all day wondering where she could find money for her next meal, before she finally swallowed her pride and called home. She had to let go of the lie that she could make it on her own. She had to admit she needed help.

PARENTS *Have to* LET GO *Too*

I (DeEtte) have had many "letting go" struggles. I continually imagined that my children would meet my expectations. Ridding myself of that tendency has been a gigantic undertaking. Let me give an example.

When my daughter Marla had completed her freshman year of college, George and I insisted that she attend a pastoral counseling center. She had exhibited significant signs of rebellion in the past and we considered this a stopgap measure to ward off any future uprising. Of course, we were naïve to believe that one week of therapy would produce a radical change. It might have, *if* it had been her idea. But she did not go happily. She was mad. She saw no need for counseling. She thought her life was fine.

I remember driving toward the center with a great deal of anxiety. With the aid and support of her counselor, Marla was supposed to confront us that day. When we entered the counseling office we saw her immediately. As beautiful as always, she looked even lovelier with a broad smile across her face. *This is good*, I thought to myself as we settled into chairs directly across from hers.

She began to tell us all she had learned that week about her family of origin and about herself. She was very honest in acknowledging the self-destructive behaviors that led to this moment. She was grateful. She asked for forgiveness. Then she began listing her complaints against us. That was fair. We were prepared.

One of the most upsetting things she discussed was her feeling that I wanted her to be like me. She emphatically stated that she was very different from me — quieter, more subdued, less expressive. My failure to accept her differences seemed to hurt her the most. I asked her forgiveness and then pledged to work at letting go of my imposed expectations and to spend more time encouraging her. We cried together, laughed, and hugged at the end of the session.

As soon as we left the office, Marla and I excused ourselves to search for the ladies' room. When we entered we were alone. I grabbed both of her hands, kind of jumped up and down, and said, "Aren't you excited? Isn't this great?" She calmly said, "Mom, you're doing it again!"

Five minutes after I had agreed to accept that she had a personality very different from mine, I was subconsciously asking her to behave like me. I wanted her to express herself as I was doing. I've had to practice — a lot! But "letting go" has made room for the joy of a better relationship with Marla.

As you pray for your child to repent and turn back to God, *you* may have some letting go to do. Maybe you are harboring bitterness and you must repent to be released of it. Do a gut-check. Be honest with yourself. Sin of any kind interferes with your ability to receive blessing. Is there anything standing between you and God's will? Are you completely surrendered? Do you believe that God knows what He is doing? What a blessing it will be when your child genuinely repents of her sin. Don't you want to be ready? Ask the Lord to shine His convicting light of truth on your spirit and show you what you have been holding too tightly. Then let go.

STEPS *to* REPENTANCE

Pray that God will call your prodigal to take each of these steps.

1. *Hear God calling.* Throughout Scripture we read that God pleads with sinners to turn from their sins. Read these examples and imagine God speaking these words to your son or daughter.

> "Turn from the evil road you are traveling and from the evil things you are doing. Only then will I let you live in this land that the Lord gave to you and your ancestors forever. Do not make me angry by worshiping the idols you have made. Then I will not harm you." (Jeremiah 25:5-6)

> "Put all your rebellion behind you, and get for yourselves a new heart and a new spirit. For why should you die, O people of Israel? I don't want you to die, says the Sovereign Lord. Turn back and live!" (Ezekiel 18:31-32)

> "As surely as I live, says the Sovereign Lord, I take no pleasure in the death of wicked people. I only want them to turn from their wicked ways so they can live. Turn! Turn from your wickedness, O people of Israel! Why should you die?" (Ezekiel 33:11)

2. *Recognize and admit sin.* Pray that the prodigal will see his sin for what it is and admit it to himself and to God. Read these promises from God and apply them to your child.

People who cover over their sins will not prosper. But if they confess and forsake them, they will receive mercy. (Proverbs 28:13)

"Only acknowledge your guilt. Admit that you rebelled against the Lord your God." (Jeremiah 3:13)

The high and lofty one who inhabits eternity, the Holy One, says this: "I live in that high and holy place with those whose spirits are contrite and humble. I refresh the humble and give new courage to those with repentant hearts." (Isaiah 57:15)

3. *Feel the pain of separation from God's love.* Pray that your child will sense that life without God is loveless. Pain is the only reason people change. Ask the Lord to use whatever pain is necessary to create a longing in your child's heart.

4. *Turn away from sin and toward God.* Pray for your child to have the courage to say goodbye to friends who encourage sinful behavior. Then ask God to help him turn his back on the past and run toward "home."

5. *Be willing to become wise with God's help.* Psalm 51:6 tells it like it is:

   But you [God] desire honesty from the heart,
   so you can teach me to be wise in my inmost being.

6. *Change.* The simplest, most difficult act required to repent is to change how one lives. Pray for your prodigal to self-correct, to change her attitudes and actions until they align with God's desire for her life. Ask God to give your child the peace that passes all understanding when she does the right thing.

Loving EVEN WHEN *It's* HARD

George and Joan have been married sixty-seven years. She has cancer. They were late to church last Sunday. He apologized to his
daughter who had waited to drive them, saying, "I am very sorry,
but I wanted to hold her a little longer before we got up." You do
not see them uncoupled. They are always holding hands or touch-
ing in some way. They are passionate about each other. He readily
confides his fear of facing life without his lifelong companion.

Their devotion is remarkable, but even more amazing is their
parenting. Each of their four children was a prodigal at a point in his
or her life, but there was never a time when the adult children
doubted how much they were loved. It had to have been very difficult for Pastor George and his wife to continually dispense unconditional love. But they did. Surprising things have happened as a
result of their steadfastness. One daughter became a full-time missionary in her fifties.

I (DeEtte) learned this lesson late. There were so many times I
didn't like my daughters and allowed this feeling to interfere with
communicating love to them. Of course, I never stopped loving
them, but there were times I failed to demonstrate how desperately
I wanted to stay connected. I was obviously conflicted and lacked
the relational skills I needed to establish a more peaceful coexist-
ence. Had I invited God into the parenting process at an earlier age,
I would have saved us all a load of grief.

I love these words from Maya Angelou: "I did what I knew how
to do, and when I knew better I did better." Today God has given
me an unlimited amount of opportunities to dispense love and
affection for my daughters, their husbands, and their children. He
has used the honesty and freedom I have found in living spiritually
connected to Him to promote understanding and acceptance in
these relationships. Many times the past will come up and I will
again express my regrets at not loving better, earlier. It's their turn

to reassure me that they indeed feel loved and cherished. My remorse is overshadowed by the joy I experience today. God had a plan and it included a lot of hurting, growing, stretching, reaching, holding, and leaning. As always, Father knows best.

PRAYER *Starter*

During your prayer time today, play background music with a repentance message—for example, "Change My Heart, O God." Imagine singing it with your prodigal beside you. Make the words of the song a prayer about your prodigal and about you. Confess any sin that has crept into your life. Thank God for the chance to repent. Commit to make changes in that area of your life.

PRAYER STRATEGIES

Surrendered heart: Always take care of your own repentance needs before interceding for your child's repentance.

Faith-builder: Think about the years it took for Austin to repent of his arrogance and unforgiveness. Remind yourself that repentance is deep work and takes time.

Persistent prayer: Choose one of the Scriptures listed under "Steps to Repentance" to pray this week. Pray it several times a day.

Written prayer: Make a list of the sins of which you hope your child will repent. Take each item and pray specifically that God would lead your child to repent of the action or attitude you wrote. Imagine sending the prayer to your son or daughter through the Holy Spirit.

Shared prayer: If you are able to communicate with your prodigal, tell him or her what you have repented of.

Chapter 11

WAITING FOR AN ANSWER

PEOPLE SEE GOD EVERY DAY — THEY JUST
DON'T RECOGNIZE HIM.
— PEARL BAILEY

You've prayed and prayed, even enlisted friends to pray. So, why hasn't there been any improvement? Is God asleep at the wheel? Did He miss your plea? Worse yet, has He simply ignored you? Impatience builds inside your body like a pacing tiger waiting to be fed, and you don't know how to pray anymore. Panic creeps in as your confidence wanes. Irritated, scared, and a little pushy, you begin to tell God what you think about His timing — it stinks!

When your daughter is living on the streets and surviving as a prostitute, or your son is becoming a Buddhist or is lost in the drug addiction cycle, you want answers to your prayers. And sooner is better than later. How disheartened we feel when we work so hard to align our own spiritual lives with Christ, yet we have no power over our child's choices or over God's intervention.

Job expressed the anguish when he said, "I cry to you, O God, but you don't answer me. I stand before you, and you don't bother to look" (Job 30:20). Of course, we know that God most definitely was looking. Job couldn't possibly have comprehended what was transpiring between God and Satan, and neither can we unless we rely on what we know about our God. We know that He is compassionate and relentless in pursuing us. He also has all the time in the universe to accomplish His goals, including that of bringing us (or our prodigal) back into an intimate, personal relationship with Him. If He isn't answering, He's saying, "Wait."

Rethinking SILENCE

The times when God seems absent or unresponsive offer the richest opportunities for stretching. In her book *Meeting God in Silence*, Sara Park McLaughlin writes, "I once heard someone pray, 'Lord, we offer you the only thing that we truly possess—our ability to be filled.'" She continues:

> All we can do is make ourselves available and open. We cannot put God in a box. No one can say with certainty what God will do, much less when and where He will do it. What I mean when I say God speaks to us in silence is that God speaks to us secretly, to the silent core of our being.[1]

Although McLaughlin is writing about our being silent, rather than God's being silent, we can apply her ideas to those times when we experience God's silence. Instead of anxiously thrashing about or shaking your fists at God, you should seek times of silent retreat to listen more closely.

I (Brendan) spent a day in a Sisters of Charity convent tucked discreetly in the center of an old industrial area of Houston. I went seeking refuge from endless stress and confusion. My hope was that I would discover what God wanted me to do about several conflicts in my life, including my resentment about my daughters' rejection of God. As I stepped into the magnificent old building, a quiet-spoken sister greeted me with a gentle smile. She explained the policy of silence upheld by all who entered and sent me to the sunlit prayer room. Leaving the gray, smog-filled air of urban life, I felt like I was in one of those movies that suddenly change from black-and-white to color. At first the silence was unnerving and the reverence glaring. But I gradually found myself smiling. Peace replaced anxiety as I relaxed into the arms of the Savior. He was everywhere. Eating lunch in silence, walking the grounds in silence, and sitting in the majestic stained-glass chapel in silence, I discovered how near God really was. He was not ignoring me or my needs. Life had just been too noisy for me to sense His presence. Within an hour I had exhausted the shopping list of things I wanted from God. So I sat and waited. Slowly, surprising thoughts began to bubble up. *Vanessa will be OK. God is working . . . trust Him. It's too soon for Natalie. Be patient.* Reassurance poured over my soul. I felt so loved and secure. Although I had no specific answers, I had assurance of God's sovereignty.

In his book *Celebration of Discipline*, Richard Foster writes:

> We live in a wordy world. All too often, we rush into the presence of God with hearts and minds askew and tongues full of words. How much better to settle down into reverential silence and awe before the Holy One of eternity.[2]

Rethink your perception of silence by viewing it as highly productive. In the 2001 issue of *Psychotherapy Research*, Heidi Levitt, a psychologist at the University of Memphis, reported that clients struggle with ways to express a new insight or to actively think about something new during periods of silence in therapy sessions. Dr. Levitt encourages therapists to facilitate these moments in spite of the awkwardness.[3] When you are in the presence of the Wonderful Counselor, you can be sure that He will use silence to speak quietly to your heart and mind. If He chooses to remain quiet, He must have a reason.

Overcoming IMPATIENCE

As you sit in silence waiting for answers, you may feel like the psalmist:

> Listen to my prayer, O God,
> do not ignore my plea;
> hear me and answer me.
> My thoughts trouble me and I am distraught. . . .
> My heart is in anguish within me;
> the terrors of death assail me.
> Fear and trembling have beset me;
> horror has overwhelmed me. (Psalm 55:1-2, 4-5, NIV)

Not knowing what to expect or do breeds a restless, impulsive, demanding attitude. Even though we are talking to the Creator of the universe, we start to sound like spoiled brats. God is not roused by impatience. He is the God of order and perfect timing.

No Pity PARTIES *Allowed*

My (Brendan's) daughter Natalie was particularly defiant during her high school and early college years. Every time I tried to guilt her into attending church with us she became more hostile. Our interactions swung back and forth between shouting matches and ice-cold silences. I prayed constantly but, more often than not, my prayers went like this: "God, why don't You listen to me? Hello! I'm talking to You! Don't You care whether Natalie goes to church?" I'm embarrassed to admit how self-centered my prayers were. The outcome I desired was positive, but my attitude stank. Receiving no apparent answer from God (those prayers didn't deserve one), I prayed less and less. I suppose I preferred to sulk. What a sullen child of the King I was! What I couldn't see was that He wanted me to trust Him to work in Natalie's life and He wanted Natalie to come to Him on her own. He wanted me to wait faithfully.

The worst part was that the longer I spent feeling sorry for myself, the more distant Natalie became. I don't blame her. Self-pity isn't pretty. Looking back, I wonder what might have happened if I had stayed patient and let the Spirit lead me. She might have been attracted to that kind of faith.

WAITING *Is* TOUGH *Work*

How many of us are good at waiting? Margie M. Lewis, author of *The Hurting Parent*, writes, "Waiting is tough work. It takes effort and a special kind of discipline of confidence."[4] Today, waiting runs counter to everything our culture emphasizes. Look around at the fast-food restaurants, drive-thru pharmacies, and high-speed modems that access online answers to almost anything in nanoseconds. The problem is that it took time for our children to get themselves into trouble, and getting them out of trouble will probably take time as well. Instant transformation is rarely genuine. Character change requires wisdom and insight that can only come by patiently sorting through painful experiences. Not only does your prodigal need time to sort out his failures, but you must wait to see what God wants to do as well.

In an article for *Pray!* magazine titled "Wrestling with Eternity," Ron Susek, an evangelist and Bible teacher, writes:

> Lack of patience implies three things: First, that you are *kinder* than God (if I were God, I'd meet this need today); second, that you think you're *smarter* than God (if I were God, I'd answer it this way); or third, that you think you're *greater* than God (I have the right to be angry with God for not answering my way).[5]

How ridiculous that we would think we are kinder, smarter, or greater than God! When God is silent, He is inviting us to listen more intently for a message that may be hard to hear.

A friend with a prodigal husband once said that she asked God why He wouldn't simply tell her whether she should wait for her husband. During her quiet time with the Lord one day she heard the Lord telling her, "Sally, if I came right into your bedroom and sat on the side of the bed and said 'This is what's going to happen,' you'd start arguing with me and tell me I ought to do it another way. That's why I'm not going to reveal the future to you until you're ready."

We like Jonathan Graf's insight into waiting on God. He writes:

> He told me to wait on Him, not like I usually did, waiting for
> someone to arrive, or for something to happen. But rather,
> wait like a waiter or waitress waits on a table . . . pen and pad
> in hand ready to listen to His words and to fill His orders—
> to serve Him.[6]

What good advice—to wait and listen for the Lord's orders and be willing to follow them with a servant's attitude.

Seize the times when you just don't feel God's presence or see Him working. Take out your pen and pad, listen alertly, and transform those times into opportunities to be still and meet the Master in the silence. He will replace the agonizing nothingness with peace, and from the peace will flow hope and a renewed focus.

KEEP *a* JOURNAL

One action you can take while waiting for God is to start a journal of your prayers for your child. Remember what DeEtte did for Layne at a turning point in Layne's life: Write something every day about Scriptures that meant something, or images you visualized, or prayers you prayed that day for your child. If your prodigal returns, give him the gift of your journal so he can grasp the love that surrounded him, no matter where he was. Then suggest that he continue to write his own prayers in it.

PRAYER *Starter*

Instead of struggling with the silence while waiting for answers, embrace it. Deliberately set up a time once or twice a week to sit in silence. Pray and listen. Write whatever thoughts come to mind.

PRAYER STRATEGIES

Surrendered heart: Is impatience filling your heart with anxiety? Empty the recycle bin. Be curious to discover what will replace the anxiety. Invite God to show you what He wants to place in your heart.

Faith-builder: Picture yourself standing on tiptoes reaching for a seldom-used item on the highest shelf. That's what you're doing in your faith right now.

Persistent prayer: Pray more, not less, when the silent times happen.

Written prayer: Keep a log of "What Silence Did for Me Today" for two weeks.

Shared prayer: Read your written prayer journal out loud to someone close.

Chapter 12

BUT IF NOT

IF IT BE SO, OUR GOD WHOM WE SERVE IS ABLE TO DELIVER US
FROM THE BURNING FIERY FURNACE, AND HE WILL DELIVER US OUT OF
THINE HAND, O KING. *BUT IF NOT*, BE IT KNOWN UNTO THEE,
O KING, THAT WE WILL NOT SERVE THY GODS, NOR WORSHIP
THE GOLDEN IMAGE WHICH THOU HAST SET UP.
— DANIEL 3:17-18, KJV, EMPHASIS ADDED

Let's face it: not every prodigal story has a happy ending. You may have done nothing to warrant your child's heading off for the life she chose. Your prayer life may be active, meaningful, and productive but not have succeeded in bringing her home yet. You are left with the question, But what do I do if she does not repent or return? The question itself is painful to ask because it implies that you have reached the end of what you can do—not a good feeling.

This chapter is about what to do when faced with what seems like failure. Nothing you have done has altered the course of your prodigal child's life. He refuses to leave the pigsty. No matter how bad the stench, he clings to his rebellion or false pride. In *Loving a Prodigal*, Norman Wright says, "One of the most devastating experiences is when the consequences of a prodigal's choices can't be reversed."[1] You have to make tough decisions regarding the rest of your life and how you will let this affect you.

A WASTED *Life:* LYDIA'S *Story*

Seven years have passed since her family last heard from Lydia. At that time she was living on the streets in New York City, prostituting to support her drug habit. She was twenty-nine years old, once beautiful, creative, and talented; but she threw all of those gifts away at a young age when drugs became her way of life.

Lydia was precocious, always ahead of her peers. Everywhere she went people responded to her beauty. She was artistic and did well in the Christian schools she attended. By eighth grade she was modeling part-time, with aspirations of being an actress or model. By fifteen, she planned to be on the cover of Vogue. Her tenacity and perseverance were her best attributes. Lydia always achieved her goals, except for keeping her father and mother together.

Her mother, Charlotte, spent four years struggling with a doomed marriage after finding out that Lydia's father preferred men. In the 1960s no one talked openly about homosexuality. Charlotte suffered in silence, afraid to tell her young daughters the real reason their parents couldn't stay together. Without enough information to understand, Lydia focused her hurt and unrelenting anger on her mother. Charlotte felt sorry for her and allowed Lydia too much power. Charlotte and her other daughter suffered Lydia's manipulation and relentless barrage of anger.

During those years, Charlotte developed a strong relationship with God, spending plenty of time on her knees begging for His mercy and comfort. She couldn't talk to anyone, except two friends, about what was happening to her family. Eventually, divorce was the only solution. She was left with her grief, her shame, and an angry daughter.

Charlotte met and married a wonderful man a year after the

divorce. Lydia refused to accept him. Two years after the second marriage, a Christian counselor decided it was time to tell Lydia the truth about her father. Charlotte had not been able to tell her. Lydia still wanted her parents to reconcile. She just wouldn't accept the divorce and tried her best to break up her mother's new marriage. She hated her mother's Christian friends and the Bible studies she attended. In Lydia's mind her mother was a "goody." Anger and disillusionment fueled her rebellious behavior.

Drug experimentation became a drug habit. During her senior year Lydia was totally out of control. She took her grandmother's car without permission. She parked it several houses down the street and began loading her belongings, intending to stay with a friend. Charlotte could tell how drugged she was. When she confronted her daughter, Lydia burst into a rage, attacking her mother like a wild animal. Charlotte called her husband and the police.

Forced into a "tough love" position, her parents knew they could not let Lydia destroy the rest of the family. Her solution was to move to her dad's. He'd been in and out of the girls' lives and saw no problem with the drugs or her friends, thinking it was a stage she'd outgrow. For two years Lydia had no direct contact with her mother or stepfather.

Lydia sank deeper and deeper into the mire of a horrendous life. Finally, after a close encounter with death, she agreed to go to a rehab program. Of course, she excelled at the program and was the number-one patient. Her mother and stepfather went to family week, during which the entire family participates in intensive therapy. Lydia's counselors all gave her rave reviews for her work, assuring Charlotte and her husband that she had tackled her problem.

Lydia tried coming home with Charlotte, but ended up returning to her dad, who was dying of AIDS. Within two months of leaving the rehab program, Lydia was back on drugs, hanging out with her old friends. Her father never grasped how serious a problem she had. Lydia covered up the truth.

Before long, Lydia introduced the family to her new love, a young man who supposedly was recovering from addictions too. They moved to New York City together, and Lydia set them up in a flat with some money she had inherited. In short order her new love took her for everything she had in order to support his habit. He died two months later. Lydia was left with nothing except another addiction—heroin.

Lydia has been in New York ever since, with long periods of total estrangement from her family and friends. They know that she's been hospitalized several times. One of those times she called and Charlotte and her sister flew there to try to bring her home. But Lydia wouldn't hear of it. She has been in prison at least three times. Police stations, morgues, hospitals, and the prison are the places her family has had to search to find her. Her outward beauty has succumbed to the scars of needles from her neck to her toes—no surface of her body has been untouched. Some of her teeth are missing due to a diet of candy. She is the epitome of Satan's seeking to devour and destroy.

Charlotte writes, "Lydia is lost, but I know the One who knows where she is. Knowing He loves her and cares for her, more than I can fathom, gives me peace. I don't know if I will ever see her again, but I trust God. I try to live only for today because my past experiences have proven that fear will ensnare me if I try to guess the future. He has only given me today. I pray for Lydia unceasingly. My wonderful sisters in Christ pray for her too. There have been times when my grief was too heavy and I just couldn't pray. At those times, I thank God for the prayer warriors that He put in my life.

"My arms would be open wide if Lydia repented and returned, just like the arms of the prodigal son's father. I long to show her the love of God. His will is always for my best, which I learn over and over. Although it is painful to walk through these valleys, God is always there to hold me and get me to the other side.

"God has given me hope in despair, peace in chaos, joy in sorrow, strength in weakness, and His abounding and everlasting love that cannot be measured. Most of all He's given me so many of His promises—and He keeps them. The prayer I have prayed for the past seventeen years is this Scripture:

> [For Lydia to] flee the evil desires of youth, and pursue right-eousness, faith, love and peace, along with those who call on the Lord out of a pure heart. [That I would not] have anything to do with foolish and stupid arguments, because [I] know they produce quarrels. As the Lord's servant [I] must not quarrel; instead, [I] must be kind to everyone, able to teach, not resent-ful. Those who oppose him [I] must gently instruct, in the hope that God will grant [Lydia] repentance leading [her] to a knowledge of the truth, and that [she] will come to [her] senses and escape from the trap of the devil, who has taken [her] cap-tive to do his will. (2 Timothy 2:22-26, NIV)

When HAVE YOU *Done* ENOUGH?

God has given your prodigal the gift of free will. Many prodigals do not return, and their families are devastated by the loss. Some die young, some stay addicted to drugs or sex, and some waste their lives. No matter how much it hurts, you must grant your child the same respect God does. And you must go on with your life.

Several years ago *Good Morning America* aired an interview of a mother whose son was a prodigal. The woman's son had become involved in the drug scene to the point that he disappeared. Fearing that he might be dead of an overdose, this mother sold her home and most of her possessions to launch a two-year search for her son. Going from crack house to crack house, she looked for him. She hired private detectives. Finally she found him and he returned home with her and entered a drug rehabilitation program. She believed she saved his life.

Most parents aren't willing to go to those extreme measures to retrieve their child, and even if they did it might not work. Again, the child has a choice. Do you wonder whether this mother went too far? The balance between going after your child and allowing God to use circumstances to bring your child to repentance is a delicate one. That's why prayer is important. Prayer leads you to wisdom.

If your child does not appear to respond to God's call, pray for wisdom to discern when to intervene and when to wait. If your child never repents or seeks God, only God can give you peace and help you to let go. I (Brendan) worked with a mother whose fifty-year-old son was addicted to marijuana and pornography, and he refused to work. This mother nearly lost her marriage because she continually bailed her son out financially, putting her own retirement resources at risk. She washed the son's clothes and frequently fed him. Her husband, the son's stepfather, became outraged, and resentment split the family. No one felt peaceful. Only when the mother established new, tighter boundaries did the son get a job. The son had no interest in changing his way of life. Without a desire to change on his part, God was left standing uninvited on the doorstep.

My counsel to this mother was that she give her energy to her marriage and pray for her son to open the door to Jesus. She struggled with ambivalence from time to time so I asked her to think of someone, real or fictional, she believed would have the strength to stand up to her son. She thought of the television courtroom show host, Judge Judy. Whenever her son would try to manipulate her, I would remind her, "What would Judge Judy do?" Immediately she sat up straighter and began to think more clearly. Sometimes it helps to have an imaginary ally.

Do WHAT YOU CAN and LET GO

The Serenity Prayer is a mere twenty-seven words: *God, grant me the serenity to accept the things I cannot change, the courage to change the things I can, and the wisdom to know the difference.* Simple concept, but so difficult to practice. If you could accomplish that kind of serenity easily, you would. Life would be a series of simple choices. But life is far from simple. You love your child more than anyone can imagine. Your identity and happiness are eternally connected to your child's welfare. Just like Lydia's mother, you will suffer a great deal if your child refuses to turn around. Respect the pain.

Surround yourself with supportive friends who are striving to know and do God's will. They can be your fueling station when you're running on empty. Go on with your life. You have to decide whether this rebellious or lost child will prevent you from experiencing joy. Don't let the tragedy contaminate all the healthy areas of your life. Give your energy to those who can receive it. God will bless that.

Prayer becomes the brace that holds you up when everything inside you wants to collapse from the strain. Commit each day to the Lord and do whatever you do for Him. He will lift you up.

Never SAY *Never*

Alexander Moya headed down the center aisle of the small church. His leg was never set properly after being shattered in an automobile accident when he was young. So he hobbled.

A persistent pastor was the reason Alexander walked that aisle. Each Saturday Pastor Billy Hill used to knock on the door of Alexander's apartment bringing a loaf of bread and an invitation to the Sunday service. Billy and his fellow church workers knocked on almost every door in the low-income apartment projects within a six-mile radius. They were not always appreciated. People slammed doors in their faces, cursed them, and hurled insults, but each Saturday the church members returned smiling, laughing, and welcoming. Alexander took the bread and one day took the invitation.

As the Spirit moved, Alexander understood Billy Hill's message from the pulpit that day. He knew it was truth. Quietly, he hobbled down the aisle and accepted a life with Jesus.

Months later his wife, Jesusa, joined him at church. Her husband was different and she wanted to know why. Sitting next to her husband, feeling his newfound strength, Jesusa listened intently as Billy Hill explained the gospel. She embraced it with her whole heart. Together, Alexander and Jesusa became faithful and diligent workers in their new church home.

They always sat by themselves in the same place, except for Mother's Day and Father's Day. On those occasions, most of their fourteen children and forty-three grandchildren joined them, but they would not be seen again until the next May. Their children refused to see the goodness of a life in Christ. They chose paths that ended in prison sentences, jail time, alcohol and drug abuse, and domestic violence. All struggled to survive financially. Alexander and Jesusa prayed for their children and grandchildren persistently. But no answer came.

One Sunday Billy Hill fought back tears as he announced that Alexander had died. Alexander's spot in the church, first seat on the right-hand side of the rear section, was empty. The small, frail man who hobbled didn't hobble anymore. He was with the One who gave him comfort and peace.

A strange thing began to happen. Each Sunday one or more of the Moya children and their families began to join Jesusa until the entire rear section of the church was filled. All fourteen children and most of the forty-three grandchildren accepted Christ. People even joke that the name of the church should be changed to Moya Mission. Moyas are everywhere, in leadership and service.

Alexander died disappointed. His family was lost. God's purpose was not fulfilled in his time—but it *was* fulfilled. A humble father's transformed life changed the future of his family even though he died unaware.

IT *Is* FINISHED!

When Reverend Dr. Dave McKechnie, senior pastor of Grace Presbyterian Church in Houston, preached a Lenten sermon on finishing, he reminded the congregation that when Jesus hung on the cross, He did not say, "I quit!" but, "It is finished!"[2] Parents of prodigals who do not return must pray for wisdom regarding when they have "finished" their work as an intercessor for their child. In some cases, parents should surrender the welfare of the prodigal to the Lord and move on with their lives until the prodigal changes. Other times parents should continue to actively intercede in the absence of any obvious change.

When in doubt, never say never—keep praying the plea for your child.

PRAYER *Starter*

Place a photo of your lost child in a private spot. Make a cup or can that has a sign taped or painted on it saying, "God Can." Whenever your prodigal is heavy on your heart, write a prayer about your concerns on a strip of paper and put it in the cup. Thank God for hearing your prayer. Periodically take the prayers out and either discard them or put them in a box. You can decide what to do with them later.

PRAYER STRATEGIES

Surrendered heart: Silently focus on the feelings you are experiencing today. Ask God to show you which ones you should let go. Consciously let them go as you exhale. Do it again, and again, until you feel clear that you have released them for today.

Faith-builder: Imagine that you are climbing the face of a huge mountain. Christ anchors the rope that is secured around your waist. He is standing at the top of the mountain, steadily holding the line until you reach Him. Can you hear Him calling to you as He reassures you of His presence? Your "mountain" is the overwhelming sadness you feel for your child. Christ will help you get beyond the pain. Trust Him.

Persistent prayer: Remember that your prayers don't have to be specific or involved. This is a marathon. Just pray every day.

Written prayer: Writing about a long-term, possibly unsuccessful intercession can be depressing. For that reason, write only once a week or once a month, or at even longer intervals. It's OK not to write about this experience all the time. Trust the Holy Spirit to let you know when something is stirring inside you. That's the time to sit down and let your thoughts flow out. Don't judge them or calculate them. Just allow a stream of consciousness to pour onto the page until you've expressed all there is. Read what you wrote and observe any themes or issues that may be important to think about or pray about.

Shared prayer: Let your friends who pray for you and your child know how much you appreciate them. Have a luncheon for them or send them a special note of thanks.

Chapter 13

TREASURES IN THE DARKNESS

AND I WILL GIVE YOU TREASURES HIDDEN IN THE DARKNESS,
SECRET RICHES; AND YOU WILL KNOW THAT I AM DOING
THIS — I, THE LORD, THE GOD OF ISRAEL,
THE ONE WHO CALLS YOU BY YOUR NAME.
— ISAIAH 45:3, TLB

Have you ever been surprised by something unexpected in the midst of a terrible experience? A kind person showed up to help when your car broke down. A check arrived at the eleventh hour to cover a payment you thought you couldn't make. You managed some valuable time alone with your spouse because the power went out in your office building. The worst failure in your career opened up a completely new career that you love. In a heated argument with your prodigal child there's a brief moment of connection — she softens the façade and you realize she cares too. These are but a few examples of the way seemingly devastating circumstances can become precious opportunities.

You have been addressing the stressful task of coping with unwanted events in your life and interceding for your prodigal child. Take a break and reflect on the priceless lessons hidden among the thorny briars of praying for your prodigal.

The WOMAN in the SAND

Mawi Asgedom, an Ethiopian exile, spent months walking in the desert searching for a refugee camp. He was only three years old when he was turned out of his village. In his book, *Of Beetles and Angels: A Boy's Remarkable Journey from a Refugee Camp to Harvard*, he recounts his most vivid memories:

> I remember our journey and the woman we met. Despite her fatigue, she walked and walked and walked, trying to limp her way to safety across miles of stones and rocks. She continued to limp, wanting to stop, but knowing that if she did, she wouldn't move again. She pressed on and on, and soon her limp became a crawl. And then I saw a sight that I would never forget—the soles of her naked feet melting away, and then disappearing into the desert, leaving only her bloody, red flesh, mixed with brownish sand and dirt. But still, she kept on limping. For what choice does a refugee have?[1]

Eventually Mawi immigrated to the United States, where he struggled to learn English and overcome cultural differences. Mawi had great difficulty understanding the abundant life in America. The first time he entered a supermarket, he cried to see so much food. He worked very hard and when he became frustrated or discouraged, Mawi remembered the woman in the sand with no shoes. If she could keep walking to get where she was going, so could he. Mawi graduated in the top 1 percent of his high school class and received scholarships to Harvard and Yale. Upon his graduation from Harvard, his class elected him to give the commencement speech. In it he credited the woman in the sand for his success. Her courage and persistence were the treasures in the darkness that had carried him so far.

The VALUE *of a* CRISIS

In *Loving a Prodigal,* Norm Wright talks about the value of a crisis: "A crisis is an opportunity for you to gain new strengths, new perspectives on life, new appreciation, new values, and a new way to approach your life. You'll look at life differently and no longer take it for granted."[2] You know this truth intellectually; it's getting it down into your very being, where the core fears reside, that's tough. God has to help you accomplish that transforming shift—when you move from knowing something is true to *knowing* in a way that changes you forever.

When you *know what you know* in the deepest places inside you, you become a new person. Any defects that may have caused you to act badly in the past disappear when you allow the light of truth to shine on them. The only way we rid ourselves of character defects is to pass through the refining fire of suffering. That is where we find the higher truths on which to base our lives. That is where we find the treasures in the darkness.

THE *Longest* AISLE

Never underestimate the possibilities in a bad experience. The most humiliating experiences with your prodigal may turn out to be the very events that set his direction later in life.

Looking back over my life, I (DeEtte) am amazed at the way God has used every painful event in my life to take me to a new level of serving Him and understanding His ways. One example is the connection between an experience I had in childhood and my calling today. When I was five and my sister was three, our mother dropped us off at church every Sunday. She didn't seem concerned about her own eternal fate, but she told us we would go to hell if we didn't attend. We each had one dress-up dress, a hat, and Sunday shoes. Often we exchanged hats to add a little variety. The church was a large Gothic structure, dark and forbidding. I felt like Dorothy approaching the great and powerful Wizard of Oz as we walked in each week. I remember the sound of my shoes on the marble floor. I held my sister's hand and dragged her toward a pew up front. Even at such a young age I was good at hiding my fear.

The people in the church never greeted us, touched us, or acknowledged that we were there. I felt invisible. That is, until we started acting up. As most unsupervised preschoolers would, we talked, laughed, argued, and often ended up in a wrestling match. People sitting around us bowed their heads, returning their concentration to the service. Some of them moved away or shushed us. Many gave us disapproving looks. They never reached out or offered to sit with us. On one occasion my sister grabbed my wide-brimmed straw hat and sailed it onto the altar, landing it right in front of the pastor. The disgruntled pastor stepped down, seized each of us by an arm, and marched us down that long aisle and out the back doors. I can still hear the click, click of my shoes as I was dragged along. He told us not to come back.

Fifty years after that awful Sunday morning, my husband and I serve in a church that ministers to children whose parents send them to church alone. Our children are greeted with love and welcomed no matter whether they behave or not. We reach out to their families and show them the love of Christ. When they walk the aisle, it is to accept Jesus as their personal Savior. Who would have thought that God would take a traumatic day in my life and use it to create a mission? He can do that in your child's life as well.

HOPE *in the* MIDST *of* SUFFERING

Chuck Swindoll writes about suffering in *Hope Again: When Life Hurts and Dreams Fade*. What a great title! Life does hurt and dreams do fade. Swindoll says, "Suffering is the common thread in all our garments." He continues:

God has given us a purpose for our existence, a reason to go on, even though that existence includes tough times. Living through suffering, we become sanctified—in other words, set apart for the glory of God. We gain perspective. We grow deeper. We grow up![3]

Swindoll offers six reasons for our hope in the midst of suffering:

1. We have a living hope. (1 Peter 1:3)
2. We have a permanent inheritance—our eternal home is secured. (1 Peter 1:3-4)
3. We have divine protection. (1 Peter 1:5)
4. We have a developing faith. (1 Peter 1:6-7)
5. We have an unseen Savior at work in unseen ways. (1 Peter 1:8)
6. We have guaranteed deliverance. (1 Peter 1:9)

Think often about these scriptural reassurances, for if you remember them you will survive the awful times along the prodigal journey. You have a dependable, durable God who cares about you. Whether your prodigal returns or not, let your suffering make you a better Christian. Let the Refiner burn out the impurities in your Christian walk. You will fulfill your calling if you do. Just as Mordecai told Esther, "Who knows whether you have come to the kingdom for such a time as this?" (Esther 4:14, NKJV).

PRUNING *Time*

One cool February morning I (Brendan) sat on the porch of a bed and breakfast called Roses and the River, watching the owner, Dick Hosack, as he pruned his beloved roses. Dick cut away so much stem and foliage that the remains seemed no more than a few stubby sticks. Certainly there was a lot more plant lying on the ground than left on the bush. The process seemed so brutal.

Dick, who had been growing roses for more than twenty years, explained that in order to ensure new growth he had to expose the core stalk to the sunlight by snipping away all of last year's growth. As the raw center of the rose bush absorbed the sunshine, it would get the nourishment it needed to bear a full bush of new and beautiful roses.

The key to your growth is allowing the light of God's truth to reach the core or center of your being. You cannot rely on last year's growth. God's grace or inspiration is wasted on you unless you cut away the old and expose the raw center of your life. That center is where you harbor hurt, fear, and bitterness. The Lord wants to take those raw, ugly feelings and transform them.

Sometimes the attitude or behavior of your children exposes your own ugliness. You lose control of your anger or resort to petty, manipulative behavior. You don't seem to be able to rise above the pull to react. Years of reacting weigh you down, blocking your path when you want to start over and do something better. God wants to prune away the obstacles. He wants to open your heart and mind to new ways of seeing and acting. You must yield to the shears in the Master's hand. Like the roses in February, your soul must be exposed to His light before it can work its wonder.

What does the Master want to prune or remove from your life? What is blocking His light? Friends who pull you into negativity? Self-indulgence? Compulsive avoidance of your problems? Take time for some honest self-examination so that you can enjoy the treasures God has for you.

An ATTITUDE of GRATEFULNESS

Patricia, a lifelong friend of mine (Brendan's), has always been a seeker. She seldom is satisfied with ordinary explanations for life's mysteries. Not long ago, she attended a conference on healing. In her small group, she met a Japanese man who told the group that he had been sent home to die of metastatic liver cancer but survived.

This retirement-aged gentleman was reserved and did not insist on talking.

When Patricia later saw him dining alone in the hotel restaurant she asked to join him. He welcomed her, and over the course of the next two hours he shared about his recovery, including how he had changed his diet to a macrobiotic regimen. Patricia asked how he managed to live with the limitations of such a restrictive diet. His response? "I am grateful for having something to eat." He then explained that the only real change he had made after receiving the terminal diagnosis was to adopt an attitude of gratefulness. He said that he deliberately remembered to be grateful for everything in his daily life, even a simple meal. He had simplified the obstacles in his life. They did not conquer him because he embraced them.

A change of perspective can make all the difference. Jesus often cut through the worries and fears of His followers, taking them to the simplest truths by encouraging them to see things God's way. God's way is not our way. Our way is to thrash around making everything complicated and to exhaust ourselves in the process. God's way is always life-giving, never anxiety-producing.

Jesus wants us to be grateful for the provision we have today and not strain to control what we cannot control. Being grateful is so simple. Why is it hard to do? A study was conducted in which people at a restaurant were asked to sit at a table where the white tablecloth had one tiny black inkstain. The food and service were impeccable, but when asked to rate the restaurant, many people commented on the stain on the tablecloth. Their eyes were so focused on what wasn't right that they couldn't appreciate what was.

In the midst of your prodigal's journey toward home, learn to be grateful for the small but positive changes that may be taking place in his or her life. Release your pent-up worry and tension to God—you'll certainly be healthier physically, emotionally, and spiritually if you do. It is hard to go around saying how grateful you are and scowl at the same time. God's splendor is often blocked by our gloom. Let's change that.

> And let the peace that comes from Christ rule in your hearts.
> For as members of one body you are all called to live in peace.
> And always be thankful. (Colossians 3:15)

It's FRIDAY — SUNDAY'S *Comin'*

Mary walked to the tomb of Jesus in utter despair. The day couldn't have felt darker. Yes, it was Sunday, but her Lord was dead, cold and rotting in that tomb. Her heart must have been heavier than the stone they rolled in front of the sepulcher. She had just spent three days weeping in inconsolable grief for this one she loved so dearly. Her mind replayed all the hopes and dreams she'd had for Him. Why didn't He stop them? How was she supposed to bear the loss? Didn't He care about her enough to find another way?

You are walking in Mary's shoes. Granted, your child is not the Messiah, but you are struggling with the darkness of loss and confusion. You don't feel God's presence. You feel alone with the pain and fear. You feel inadequate. And you are. You cannot bring your prodigal home — it's up to him. You may feel grateful for the blessings, but what about the dark future?

She felt a gentle tap on her shoulder and heard someone say her name: "Mary." Startled, she turned from the bleakness of the tomb and recognized Him. Sunday wasn't dark anymore. He had risen! He came back! Joy flooded the riverbanks of despair. Tears flowed — a mix of bitter and sweet. Mary would spend her whole life pondering this moment; but what a moment it was! She didn't know how this resurrection came about, but she witnessed it with great excitement. Darkness turned to joy in the instant of Christ's return. No matter how many times He had tried to explain to His disciples what would happen, they couldn't get it. We are like the disciples: We hear the promises of resurrection and hope, but we just don't see it.

College professor and author Dr. Anthony Campolo tells about a rousing sermon given by his pastor, who stood before the congregation and shouted, "It's Friday—but Sunday's comin'." The pastor repeated those words over and over until the congregation began chanting them with him. "It's Friday—but Sunday's comin'. It's Friday—but Sunday's comin'." Slow to catch on but excited once they did, these people felt the presence of the Living Hope. They felt the reassurance of Jesus' power to conquer death. The animated pastor imprinted on their hearts the message that Christ will not leave us or forsake us.[4]

As you navigate the darkness, listen for Jesus calling your name. He wants you to know that He is there. He will reassure you of His steadfast love. Sunday's comin'.

GO *on a* TREASURE *Hunt*

We hope to have convinced you to take another look at the suffering you endure because of your prodigal's actions. When Isaiah wrote that there are treasures hidden in secret places, we don't know for sure what he meant, but we have an idea. The kind of character-building lessons that shape who we are, that change our identity, most often happen in a context of pain. Humans rarely change without first experiencing pain. The challenge is to stop running from the pain and start embracing it as a chance to grow. Seek the knowledge that will develop new strength or new faith in you.

When Adam and Eve ate the fruit from the Tree of Knowledge they gave up innocence in exchange for wisdom. You have given up innocence in relation to your child, but have you exchanged it for wisdom? If you stay stuck in bitterness or fear, you miss the gift of wisdom. Wisdom involves knowing the truth about yourself, being humble. Wisdom means recognizing that God is actively working in your life and calling you to integrity. You will find integrity when you accept your weaknesses and allow God to transform them into strengths. You will find integrity in the secret places of the soul where only you and God may enter.

PRAYER *Starter*

Pray for Mawi Asgedom and others who teach us to be thankful for the blessings we take for granted.

PRAYER STRATEGIES

Surrendered heart: Talk to the Lord about the darkness. Tell Him whether you can see the treasures in secret places. You have only to be willing.

Faith-builder: Do you remember an incident with your prodigal that seemed completely bleak and then God turned things around? Or can you see a characteristic in someone that came only as a result of his suffering or failure?

Persistent prayer: If you can't find a silver lining in the clouds surrounding you, ask God to show you one. Ask again.

Written prayer: Make a list of everything you are grateful for. Give praise in your prayers for those gifts.

Shared prayer: Tell someone else the things you are grateful for. Thank a prayer partner for being there for you.

Part Four

HOMECOMING

Chapter 14

GAINING A NEW PERSPECTIVE

Does your prodigal leave you feeling a bit insane at times? Do you wonder what is real and what is imagined? How easy it is to become paranoid over even the hint of a problem when you have a troubled child. After a while you don't know what or whom to trust. You aren't sure God is alert enough to handle your child's increasingly clever ability to self-destruct. You need perspective.

One of the slogans of Alcoholics Anonymous is "Sanity is perspective." The wisdom of those words comes from years of members sharing stories that could make your hair curl. The truth is, we need two kinds of perspective: insight into ourselves as well as a bigger view of our child's life.

We lack insight when we react and defend ourselves rather than taking time to figure out what we feel or need. If you slowed down and asked yourself, "What's really hurting or scaring me?" you might be surprised by the answer. Once you grasp the underlying feelings that triggered a reaction, solving the problem before you is much easier. Be willing to look at your own reactions and try to "connect the dots." In other words, figure out why certain behaviors set you off more than others. It could be that you react more to feeling inadequate, or that situations where you feel disrespected really hit your hot button. Discover your sensitive spots.

Another perspective problem is *spiritual myopia,* or nearsightedness. We get so caught up in our prodigal's perpetually bad judgment and the fallout from it that we can't see beyond the present. The reality that our children will probably live a long life and have many opportunities to change gets lost in the emotion of the experience. Lee Iacocca is quoted as saying, "We are continually faced by great opportunities brilliantly disguised as insoluble problems."

CAST *the* VISION

On a recent vacation my (Brendan's) family decided to work on a jigsaw puzzle together. Cardboard pieces covered the entire surface of the card table. As we began to sort them, we first looked for corner pieces, followed by easily identifiable sections. Then came the painstaking task of staring and staring at the rest of those color-splashed puzzle pieces, wondering if we'd ever successfully reconstruct the picture on the box cover.

Have you had this experience? Do you remember the moment when you found the final piece? You were ecstatic as you pushed its perfect shape into the manufacturer's design. Voilà! A beautiful picture. Before you felt that excitement, you had to thoughtfully visualize the end product. You had to "see" it in your mind's eye. Golfers are taught this same principle. Jack Nicklaus always says that as you stand on the fairway you should "see" the exact flight of the ball and its safe landing on the green before playing the actual stroke.

Thanks to your rebellious child, you need a similar strategy. Your son or daughter has dumped all the "pieces" of his or her life in a disarray of confusing behaviors, emotions, and attitudes. Although you are not the one putting the puzzle together, you may be the one who can "see" what no one else can. You may be the one who can picture the path your prodigal will travel to come home. The strangest truth about the prodigal's journey is that in spite of how long a detour he seems to take, sometimes it is the shortest route for him to reach the goal.

God may want to use you, the parent, to create and suggest a vision for the path of your child's return to faith. You may "see" the green and point the way for a safe landing. Your vision of what is possible may be what sustains *you* while you wait and it may transform your child's image of himself.

Remove OBSTACLES

Look inside yourself and discover the obstacles blocking your view. Ask the all-knowing God to reveal any trouble spots to you so that you may work on them. Sometimes the prodigal isn't the one who is "off"—it's the family who is "off."

I (Brendan) worked with a family who brought their twenty-two-year-old in for counseling. The parents and both sets of grandparents attended the session, fully expecting me to set their prodigal straight about her choice of friends. As they sat and talked through their feelings, I realized that the family wasn't giving this young woman a chance to be treated as an adult. Basically, they wanted to continue managing her life for her rather than allowing her to grow up. She might not have been making the best choices, but at twenty-two, she needed to know that she was free to make those choices and to suffer any consequences.

These well-meaning relatives needed insight into what they were doing. They needed to understand that God gives all of His children the freedom to choose, and families should too. How many of us gained the wisdom we have by never making a mistake? The other thing this family needed was to realize that this young woman had many chapters of her life yet to live. They acted as if what was happening now was the last chapter, her last chance to become the person God wanted her to become.

GAIN a HEART of WISDOM

Psalm 90 captivated us when we began to pray for our daughters. Verse 12 says, "Teach us to number our days aright, that we may gain a heart of wisdom" (NIV). We like the expression "a heart of wisdom" because wisdom begins in our hearts. Our heads rationalize, justify, and defend us when we are scared or sad, but honesty is found in the heart. Core truths are often described as being at "the heart of the matter." In order to "number our days aright" we need to see things the way God sees them. That requires us to give up our puny plans and be curious about His. Once we give up our emotional investment in getting the outcome we want, as opposed to the outcome God has planned, we are free to explore the possibilities.

If we pursue a "heart of wisdom" instead of a perfect ending to our story, God will reveal Himself in all His splendor. Sometimes the most splendid thing God does is to give us peace during the impossible times—to quiet our spirits when we dread every phone call, to hold us close when we don't know what to do. Other times He supernaturally lets us know what to say or when to say it during those rare opportunities with our prodigal. No matter how God reveals His splendor, we must see it with our heart even though it's natural to harden it in defense against pain. Your heart will respond to the Lord's instruction if you keep it open. Pray for Christ to soften the hard places deep within you.

BLESS *the* TRIALS

The bigger view is easier to see looking backward than facing forward. Yet as Christians we are called to live in the kingdom of God in the present with an understanding that God is working all things together for good.

Alexander Solzhenitsyn, the great Russian dissident imprisoned for his writing, said, "It was only when I lay there on rotting prison straw that I sensed within myself the first stirring of good. . . . So, bless you prison for having been in my life."[1]

What if you blessed the trials you are suffering today? What if you thanked God for making you a better person through this adversity? And what if you thanked Him for using any means necessary to build in your son or daughter the character needed for kingdom living?

VICTORY *Is* WON *in* INCHES

The famous western novelist Louis L'Amour said, "Victory is won in inches. Win a little, hold your ground, and win a little more."[2] As you pray for your prodigal you need a kingdom perspective, one that allows you to think in terms of eternal victories. Pray for "inches" of gain toward the goal of your prodigal's turning around and seeking a relationship with Christ.

My (Brendan's) daughter Natalie is still not sure what kind of faith she wants. She is intrigued by the mystique of other religions and frustrated with my efforts to change her thinking. But we sit and talk. We no longer yell and scream at each other. She doesn't call me a "Branch Davidian" (a religious cult that made lots of headlines) anymore just because I go to church so often. I believe that Natalie knows Christ and I pray that she will choose to fellowship with Him someday. In the meantime, I'm thankful that the doors of communication are open.

RECOGNIZE *His* DEEDS

Satisfy us in the morning with your unfailing love,
that we may sing for joy and be glad all our days.
Make us glad for as many days as you have afflicted us,
for as many years as we have seen trouble.
May your deeds be shown to your servants,
your splendor to their children. (Psalm 90:14-16, NIV)

Do you realize that God's love doesn't fail? You may fail to grasp it or embrace it, but that doesn't change the reality. The psalmist begged God to satisfy him in the morning and make him glad for the same length of time he was sad. Apparently the psalmist believed that God would grant such a request.

Maybe God included this passage in His Word to show us that, in spite of the pain and sorrow we endure with our prodigals, He can give us joy again. Joy? How could you ever feel glad after suffering so much? One way is to start noticing all the subtle and not-so-subtle ways the Lord intervenes in your life and in your child's life. When the invisible becomes visible, you'll rejoice. Your perspective will change. You'll no longer feel alone or helpless and you'll move forward with assured confidence that God is in control. He is directing your child to every possible opportunity for repentance and transformation. All you have to do is pray for her to recognize His splendor when she sees it. Nothing can compare.

As you take inventory of the Master's deeds in your life or your child's life, write them down in a prayer journal. Where have you seen His touch? Was it the amazing timing of a chance meeting between your child and a godly friend? How about the provision of money for counseling when you couldn't possibly afford it? Or what about the prayer support of your church? An author friend, Elise NeeDell Babcock, who wrote the book *When Life Becomes*

Precious, encourages people in difficult circumstances to keep a "victory journal."[3] She tells them to record three victories every day for thirty days, whether small or large. By doing so, you may begin to realize just how active He is in your life.

GOD *Is* EVERYWHERE

When my (Brendan's) daughter Vanessa was living in Germany with her young husband who didn't have much interest in the Lord at the time, I prayed daily that God would bring godly friends into their lives. One day, Vanessa called with the news that Drew had been invited to attend a Promise Keepers rally in a nearby town. The reality that Promise Keepers had spread to Europe was stunning for me. I had no idea that Drew would be exposed to such a mighty Christian men's movement, but God knew. He had planned that Drew would go to that event. Jehovah Jireh, the Hebrew name of God that means "the LORD will provide" (Genesis 22:14), was working a small miracle. Realizing the limitless ability of God, I embraced a bigger view of what God could do in Vanessa and Drew's lives, and my perspective changed. Instead of believing that they were wasting time living in a far land, I began to realize that God was there too.

If we can grasp the vastness of our Lord's resources and power, we can trust that our prayers will be answered. Even as we desperately pray for Him to intervene in a certain way, we must comprehend that He may be using what seems impossible to bring about a greater goal in our child's life.

Think KINGDOM THOUGHTS

Tears streamed down my face, so I (Brendan) could hardly see to drive. The world seemed surreal. I was driving away from the hospital where my father's body lay cold and gray. Two hours before, he had died from a sudden heart attack. I struggled to comprehend the finality of my loss. Many times in my life I had actually wished he would die. His alcoholism had taken him from me at an early age. I resented the loss of connection with him when he chose the bottle over life. He believed that alcohol gave him the confidence that he needed to succeed as a salesman. However, in the last three years of his life he had stopped drinking. He never talked about it, but we had our dad back. He was fun and loving. He returned to the faith of his youth. I wasn't ready for him to go.

As I drove home, trying to grasp what had just happened, I experienced a brief but powerful vision of a twelve-year-old boy running though a field totally carefree. The boy in my vision was dressed in overalls like boys might have worn in the 1930s (when my father would have been that age). I had never thought of such an idea before. The image lasted only a few seconds. The timing of this wide-awake dream puzzled me. Then it hit me. God, in all His graciousness, had shown me a glimpse of where my dad was at that very moment. This man whom I dearly loved was in heaven. He was free. He had run away from home at fourteen and married by nineteen. Most of his life had been spent worrying and burdened by the responsibility of a large family.

Twelve years old was probably the last time he had been carefree. How awesome that God would give my dad the new body of a carefree little boy! I laughed. The pain of my grief melted away. A calm sense of trust in the Lord filled me. He had noticed my tears and sent relief.

I want my children to remember that the Lord loved their grandfather and that, in spite of Papaw's prodigal behavior, He was faithful. He gave my dad the joy he couldn't quite find on earth. God's mercy endures forever. When we belong to God, He knows our pain. He probably wanted my father to enjoy his life here as much as that boy in my vision enjoyed his romp through heavenly fields.

I wonder how often we miss the joy and the freedom planned for us in eternity. How amazing that God holds the blessing for us until we are ready to receive it. If we could teach our children to picture God holding their blessings, waiting for them to claim them, maybe they would discover who the Creator intended them to be. Maybe that's what "thy kingdom come" means. We can live as if we have already arrived in heaven and received the gifts our heavenly Father has chosen for us.

Pray that God will give you a glimpse of the blessings He is holding for you and for your child. These words of the apostle Paul can help:

Yet what we suffer now is nothing compared to the glory he will give us later. For all creation is waiting eagerly for that future day when God will reveal who his children really are. (Romans 8:18-19)

And even we Christians, although we have the Holy Spirit within us as a foretaste of future glory, also groan to be released from pain and suffering. We, too, wait anxiously for that day when God will give us our full rights as his children, including the new bodies he has promised us. Now that we are saved, we eagerly look forward to this freedom. For if you already have something, you don't need to hope for it. But if we look forward to something we don't have yet, we must wait patiently and confidently. (Romans 8:23-25)

RELAX *and* ENJOY *the* PROCESS

"The Power of Houston" is an annual extravaganza hosted by many of the city's businesses. Fireworks and gigantic laser shows are part of the entertainment, but the most fascinating performance is that of a group of skydancers called Bandaloo. These agile, daring men and women dance high above the city streets on ropes attached to skyscrapers, bouncing off the buildings as they twist and twirl. Onlookers watch in awe.

A friend of ours, Kelli, happened to work in one of these high-rises. For two weeks prior to the show, Bandaloo practiced outside her twelfth-floor office windows, bouncing back and forth. They also used Kelli's window to enter the building. In August, when all this was going on, Houston temperatures were daily reaching the triple digits, and the 100 percent humidity intensified the heat.

Kelli had been suffering from anxiety due to money problems, family relationships in conflict, and chronic pain. She didn't need any more stress. Yet she found herself sitting by an open window while these performers rehearsed. The open window meant the air conditioning was useless. She sweated profusely all day as people would walk by and invariably comment, "Does it seem a little warm in here to you?"

To top it all off, every so often the dancers would come sailing through her window strapped in their harnesses, revealing their "privates" as the wind blew their shorts. She found that all she could do was laugh.

In fact, due to the sheer absurdity of the entire experience she couldn't stop laughing for two weeks. Oddly enough, her physical pain eased, and her worries took on a new perspective.

Laughter transports us from our worries. We need laughter, especially when terrible things are happening in our lives. If we walk around depressed and glum all the time, our bodies will get sick from a lack of endorphins and other natural mood elevators. One thing I (Brendan) tell clients who are overly stressed is to rent a comedy movie and allow themselves to get lost in the silliness in order to relax those hard-to-reach spots in the psyche.

I (Brendan) once taught a class on parenting teens that came with reminder cards to hand out each week. The card that helped the parents the most shared this reminder: *Relax and enjoy the process.* What they liked about it was the simple instruction to view what was happening with their children as a process, not a final product. If they could ease up, worry less, and enjoy the fact that God is in control, they would be better parents. I stuck that card on my own bathroom mirror and read it every day.

As parents of prodigals, like Kelli on the twelfth floor we must find ways to relax and enjoy the strange experience in which we find ourselves. When we do, we will receive a surprising benefit—release. As James writes, "Consider it pure joy, my brothers, whenever you face trials of many kinds, because you know that the testing of your faith develops perseverance" (James 1:2-3, NIV).

PRAYER *Starter*

Imagine stepping out of your self and hovering up near the ceiling. Observe your attitude, posture, and speech as you talk to others about your prodigal. Become aware of what you seem to believe about the situation. Are you depressed? Hopeful? Ask God to give you a new perspective as you look at the dilemmas overwhelming you today. Stay open.

PRAYER STRATEGIES

Surrendered heart: Are you willing to relinquish your perspective if it gets in the way of God's plan?

Faith-builder: What would you think if God told you that your child would absolutely benefit from these trials?

Persistent prayer: Are you discouraged? Pray in a different place or posture today.

Written prayer: Write what you think your perspective has been, then ask God to guide you as you write what you sense His Holy Spirit is revealing to you.

Shared prayer: Ask two people how they would interpret what has happened recently in your family. Thank God for others' points of view.

Chapter 15

PREPARING FOR
THE RETURN

WE GIVE OUR LIVES BACK TO YOU.
WILL YOU TAKE US INTO YOUR ARMS ONCE AGAIN?
FORGIVE US FOR TURNING AWAY.
WILL YOU HELP US TO STAY WHERE LOVE NEVER ENDS?
—SONG LYRICS BY ALLISON ASH[1]

What will your child's homecoming be like? Picture yourself as the father in Jesus' parable. As you stand on the road, looking off in the distance, and see your prodigal's silhouette, you immediately begin planning the celebration. You gather the robe, the sandals, and the ring.

What will *your* robe, sandals, and ring be? These objects, described in Luke 15:22, symbolize the nature of the new relationship you are offering this child who once was lost. Maybe you'll throw your arms around your son and offer him the comfort of love and forgiveness. Better yet, you might help him shed the dirty reminders of his journey and trade them for the fresh, clean shoes of new opportunities to help him stand firm on solid ground. The ring? How will you return the symbol of belonging and importance to this wayward son? These symbolic moments etch themselves into the hardened places of the spirit. Rituals mark important turning points or passages in our lives. As you prepare for your prodigal's return, pray for wisdom regarding how to mark this long-awaited event.

Be AWARE of Your EXPECTATIONS

"Coming home" has so many meanings. First and foremost, you hope that your child will return to a relationship with God. In the parable the father embraced the son before he washed off the filth. He didn't know what shape his son was in; he just knew that he had returned of his own free will. It is hoped that your prodigal will return to relationship with you and the family as well as with God, but these two parts of the return may not occur simultaneously. Don't expect a complete return overnight.

CHANGE Isn't EASY

I (DeEtte) was thirty-eight years old the first time I held a Bible in my hands. My world turned inside out and upside down when I began my spiritual journey. I had erected impenetrable barriers to prevent any chance of exposure to a god outside myself. I didn't need anything or anybody. I was self-contained.

But God changed me! He exposed the emptiness and barren waste that was my life. I think I know how Eve must have felt when she stood naked before the Creator. I felt uncovered and unmasked. It wasn't a Damascus experience; my changes were slow. I gradually released my grip on all the things I had clung to for significance and worth. Without the façade to protect me, I faced the damage and rubble of our family life.

Although married and the mother of three daughters, I was career-obsessed and performance-driven and led a separate life from my husband and children. My children had known only stress and conflict. I hadn't been a real mother, and we only loosely met the definition of "family." The way we functioned in our early years set into motion the problems that would surface later when our daughters took the prodigal path. By the time I let God in, I had already taught them how to live life. I was changing horses midstream and expecting them to follow, while they were content to ride the old one. As God drew me closer, my children moved farther away, to their version of the "far country." Their lives reflected the self-centered values I had shown them. Our journey toward each other has taken a long time. Whenever I want them to grow spiritually, I am reminded to be as patient with my children as God was with me.

RESPECT *the* PRODIGAL'S WILL

The father in the parable was unequivocally excited and expressive about his son's return. Therefore, we believe it's fair to say that God wants you to celebrate your child's homecoming. The catch is to be sure that your actions are focused on the decision made by your child, not on *your* needs. Absolute respect for the prodigal's freedom to choose his own path is necessary to keep from smothering him when he "comes home." The father may have appeared to take over once the son arrived, but remember that the son was asking to be accepted as a servant. The father merely returned his son to full relationship status as a sign of forgiveness and love. He didn't force his will on the son. Your job is to offer love and acceptance if your child is willing to receive it. If not, you may have to "wait in the road" a little longer until your prodigal sets his sights on God and navigates the remaining obstacles.

The LONG WAY *Home*

The phone rang, and Beth answered. "Hello?"

"Can I come over and talk with you? *Now?*" Don, her son-in-law of five months, sounded unusually worried.

"Of course, come on over." Beth looked at her husband, Wayne, with a confused expression. Last night they had enjoyed a lovely evening with the newlyweds, watching the Olympic cycling trials at the velodrome. Beth recalled thinking that all was well even though she and her daughter, Rebecca, had not always enjoyed this kind of relationship. Rebecca and Beth had frequently been estranged due to Rebecca's alcohol abuse, deceit, and betrayal, but that was in the past. Beth felt peaceful and content that they had weathered the rough spots and were headed for calmer sailing, especially now that Rebecca and Don were happily married.

A few minutes later, Don arrived and they ushered him into the sitting room, curious to discover what prompted this visit. The next words spoken shattered their world.

"Rebecca's gone," Don blurted. "She's moved out." The words didn't make sense. Surely they had heard wrong.

"What are you talking about? What do you mean?" But even as Beth spoke, the panic began overtaking her.

"She wasn't going to tell you until after you returned from vacation. She has moved in with another man — a man she met at work."

Beth gasped as if the wind had been knocked out of her. She refused to accept what she was hearing. There had to be another explanation. This was crazy! She didn't remember much of what happened after that. Wayne reassured Don that they would talk with Rebecca.

They called their daughter and asked to see her immediately. At first she refused; then she relented. When she arrived her face was chiseled in defiance. Wayne and Beth desperately reminded Rebecca of the vow she'd taken before God. She didn't waver. They begged her to seek counseling. She didn't waver. They pleaded with her to wait and attempt to work things out with Don. She didn't waver. The stone façade could not be penetrated. Her heart, hardened by stubborn self-will, walled her off from her parents' words, their concern, and their judgment. She left angry.

Beth and Wayne sat stunned, staring at the empty space where Rebecca had sat. They didn't know the person she had become. Where was the twelve-year-old girl who had given her heart to Jesus at church camp? Where was the fourteen-year-old who had dragged her entire family to church and altered their lives forever? Where was the seventeen-year-old who had trekked up a mountain during a wilderness experience and proclaimed an unbelievable closeness to her Creator?

They felt as if they had watched their daughter die. All the hopes and dreams were shattered, and the despair was overwhelming. Beth and Wayne held each other and wept. Finally, they surrendered their grief and pain and helplessness to God.

Over the next week they pieced together what had happened. Rebecca had met a man named Ahmed while working for a large computer firm. Before she married Don, Ahmed tried to persuade her to change her plans, but Rebecca couldn't bring herself to cancel the wedding. She believed she could end her relationship with Ahmed.

After the wedding Rebecca started drinking heavily and staying out late, telling Don that she was working overtime or going out with the girls when she was actually meeting Ahmed. She avoided her parents. With the aid of alcohol she mustered the courage to file for a divorce.

Months later Rebecca used the excuse of needing medical insurance information to call her parents. Beth and Wayne sensed that Rebecca missed the relationship with them but didn't know how to reconnect. Her shame was in the way. When they heard that she was in the hospital with a serious infection, they rushed to see her. As they entered the hospital room they literally ran into Ahmed. Wayne and Beth were polite but distant and obviously felt awkward. Everything about Rebecca's present life ran counter to their values and seemed to be a slap in the face of God. For a year after the hospital encounter, Rebecca stayed away from her mom and dad until she and Ahmed decided to marry. Beth and Wayne again pleaded with Rebecca and with God. They couldn't accept the life she was choosing.

Choking back their disappointment, Beth and Wayne reached out to Ahmed and he eventually began to return their affection. But Beth challenged Ahmed, pointing out the tremendous differences between him and Rebecca in culture and religion (he was Muslim). She asked him how he would tolerate her telling his children that Jesus was the only way to truth and spirituality. She made clear that she would not be silent. Ahmed didn't take her seriously. He felt sure they could "work it out." Beth wished she knew what God had planned. She had no idea what lay ahead.

Only weeks later, Beth and Wayne's phone rang in the middle of the night. It was Rebecca, screaming.

"He's going to kill me! Help me!"

Beth was horrified, her worst nightmare realized. Although she was scared for Rebecca's safety and wanted to help her out of the relationship, she knew that a rescue mission would only have a temporary effect.

So Beth said, "Call the police. Don't call us. Call the police."

Hanging up the phone, Beth woke her husband and they prayed with renewed intensity. They prayed until the sun came up and prayed some more.

A few days later Rebecca moved out of the apartment she shared with Ahmed and into her parents' home, afraid of what Ahmed might do. Beth and Wayne agreed, on the condition that Rebecca would go to counseling and attend AA meetings.

Rebecca's journey back to God took years. Eventually, she met and married a man who loved God with all his heart, and they now have four children. Beth and Wayne received answers to their prayers beyond what they had asked. God held the gift of a much better life for Rebecca until she was ready to claim it.

How DO I TRUST *the* RETURN?

Beth and Wayne thought Rebecca had returned and all was well; then Rebecca unleashed a whole new set of problems. Many of the parents we interviewed for this book told similar stories. Although you may be among those who enjoy a once-and-for-all repentance, return, and reconciliation, we offer these stories to prepare you for the possibility that your prodigal's return may take a long time — with a few stops and starts along the way. What is important is that you take one scenario at a time. Elisabeth Eliot, a writer and radio host who lost her first husband at the hands of a primitive tribe in Ecuador, frequently advises callers to her program to "just do the next thing." As you and your child walk through the experience of returning, just do the next thing — whatever that requires.

More THAN ONCE: *a* FATHER'S *Story*

Jeff went away to college and after his freshman year came home an alcoholic. He had flunked out of his classes, lost twenty pounds, and sold his stereo and hunting rifle. He told his father Mark he was drinking a fifth of whiskey every day and that he blacked out often.

Jeff knew the prevalence of alcoholism in his family. Mark had warned him, but Jeff's grandfather had given him his first drink — a confusing message, to be sure. He started drinking heavily during high school. Fearful of the danger of alcohol, Jeff tried marijuana. When using marijuana, he had no fear of alcohol. After Jeff admitted all this, Mark told him, "You know you're an alcoholic." Jeff answered, "Yes. And I'm willing to do whatever I need to do to get help."

Mark wondered how Jeff could have been drinking in high

school right under their noses. Every time he came in after a night out, Mark or Jeff's mom, Ann, would make him stand face-to-face with one of them. They subtly but deliberately would smell his breath, but because Jeff knew that vodka didn't have an odor, he was able to maintain his drinking and his secret too. Lying about what he was doing or who he was with became part of the game. Mark and Ann had underestimated the resourcefulness of a prodigal.

But that was history; Jeff had come home. He was humble and repentant. He began counseling with a Christian psychologist and attended Alcoholics Anonymous meetings. A strong Christian friend of Mark's with thirty years of sobriety even volunteered to accompany Jeff to his first meeting. Mark took an upbeat approach with his son, saying things like, "You can do this." "I'm so proud of you for your recovery." Inside he was devastated.

Mark's father had been an alcoholic and Mark had done everything he knew to break the cycle. He never used alcohol. Dealing with his own despair was as hard as helping his son.

Jeff made great progress. Soon he was helping other young adults in their recovery. He even became a counselor for an organization that helped teens and young adults find their way out of addiction. After five years of sobriety he married a beautiful young woman who worked for the same group. They became active in a church with a special ministry to people from families with addictions. Mark and Ann thought their son's prodigal story had ended.

However, less than two years into the marriage, things began to unravel. Jeff's wife had unresolved issues, and he was immature. In one fight, she threw a ten-pound object at him, bashing a wall of their apartment. He relapsed and started drinking. She kicked him out. Searching for a place to stay, Jeff moved into a men's home for the city's down-and-outers. When Mark and Ann went to see him they were shocked.

Jeff and his wife tried to reconcile, but their relationship continued to deteriorate. She refused to go to counseling even though she was a counselor herself. He relapsed again, and she kicked him out of the house a second time. A divorce followed.

Several months later Mark and Ann were traveling, staying with friends in another state. Jeff tracked them down at 2 A.M., saying he needed to go to a treatment center for help. His parents could hardly believe their ears when he explained that he was addicted to cocaine.

Mark and Ann decided on a drug treatment center and put Jeff on a plane. This time his troubles had gotten geometrically worse. Alcoholism seemed like an easy problem compared to cocaine. Indeed, though Jeff recovered and came home, within weeks he had relapsed again. Mark and Ann had to learn the hard way that prodigals often have to try more than once, and that sometimes the way to help them is to not welcome them home. That hurt.

Today Jeff is sober and is putting his life back together one day at a time. Mark, too, celebrates a day at a time, realizing he must be careful not to give his son what he can get for himself. Mark's boundaries are in place. He loves Jeff but does not let that love keep him from making tough decisions. The Parable of the Prodigal Son has not lost its power or beauty for Mark. He has even more admiration for the model of God's love and forgiveness that the story portrays. The Father forgives even when He has been used and rejected. Not only does He forgive, He rejoices.

PRACTICE *the* FULL POWER *of the* CROSS

Mark didn't give up on the possibility of Jeff's return to healthy spiritual living, but he also realized that he must walk with his son through the brokenness. Have you considered that God is walking with you every time you have to make a critical decision about your prodigal? Denise Glenn, founder of Mother Wise and author of *Freedom for Mothers*, writes:

To fully realize the power of the cross, you must align your will with the Father's in that critical time and place where there will be a crucifixion moment of decision. You have an opportunity to practice the full power of the cross each day as you walk in brokenness with God, with those in your family, and with the world. The presence of the cross in your life will be revealed in the window of your eyes and the glow on your face. The awesome power of the cross will reach beyond you into the hearts and lives of those who will see it in your life and be forever changed.[2]

Preparing for your prodigal's return may mean finding the power of the cross in your everyday life. Beth and Wayne refocused on their marriage and their service to others during the dark times when Rebecca was far from them emotionally and spiritually. They couldn't speed up her return so they sped up their spiritual growth. That's what you have to do when the timing of the return doesn't make sense to you. It doesn't mean there will not be a return; it means God wants to accomplish preliminary victories. Be willing to lay the groundwork for a successful return.

REST UP *to Be* READY

The only light in the small theater was a spotlight illuminating the young male performer dressed in the Bavarian costume of Captain von Trapp. His voice was both strong and soft as he sang a moving rendition of *Edelweiss*. Keaton, my (DeEtte's) four-year-old grand-daughter, had reached the limit of her attention span. I sat up straight, trying to adjust to a more comfortable position on the hard-surfaced ledge where I'd been sitting for two hours. My hands were loosely crossed in my lap when my granddaughter reached over and, rather forcefully, moved my hands to the side. She acted as if she owned her grandmother's lap, because she does.

My grandchildren have full access to my lap. Available, inviting, and comfortable, my lap is a place where they know they are welcome anytime. When they choose to climb up, they will always find love.

God's comfort and safety is like that. He gives us permission to climb onto His lap any time, any place. How wonderful to know that all we have to do is reach out and He will pull us toward Him and let us *rest*. Sometimes we need a rest from the battering blasts of disappointment and fear.

In *The Great House of God*, Max Lucado writes about the secret to finding land in a storm: "You don't aim at another boat, you don't stare at the waves—you set your sight on an object unaffected by the wind—a light on the shore—and go straight towards it."[3] The reason to be "rested" spiritually is so that you can become the unaffected object for your child. When Peter stepped out of the boat and began walking on the water, he needed to focus on Jesus. Your prodigal needs to be able to look to you because you believe she can make it. As your prodigal turns toward home she will experience resistance from within and without. She will take her eyes off the goal. If you're ready, you can offer her a consistent beacon of love and safety. Pray that she will aim for it.

Be PRAYED *Up*

Preparing yourself for your prodigal's return isn't easy. You may sense that she's ready to return, but *you* are still harboring resentment. That is why you must spend soul-searching time in prayer about any obstacles in your own path. Are you hurt because your prodigal said cruel words before he left? Is the shame burdening you to the degree that you cannot look at your child without remembering everything bad that's happened? What about your fear? Are you terrified that she will relapse and you don't think you could survive another round? You'll know that you are ready when you can truly don the "clothing" described in Colossians 3:12-15. Listen to this passage to understand the goal of reconciliation:

> Since God chose you to be the holy people whom he loves, you must clothe yourselves with tenderhearted mercy, kindness, humility, gentleness, and patience. You must make allowance for each other's faults and forgive the person who offends you. Remember, the Lord forgave you, so you must forgive others. And the most important piece of clothing you must wear is love. Love is what binds us all together in perfect harmony. And let the peace that comes from Christ rule in your hearts. For as members of one body you are all called to live in peace. And always be thankful.

The psalmist said, "Thy word is a lamp unto my feet, and a light unto my path" (Psalm 119:105, KJV). Ask the Lord to light your path as you check for unresolved feelings. As discussed in an earlier chapter, there's nothing wrong with what you feel; it's what you do with the feelings that matters. If your feelings continue to divide you and your child, spend more quiet time with the Lord and allow Him to guide you.

STAY *in the* PRESENT *and Be* PATIENT

You may have to work through "unfinished business" that exists between you and your prodigal after his return. Realize that his return does not mean that he's totally in tune with God or you. He probably has plenty of inner conflicts and bad habits to change. Remember the old bumper sticker that read, "Be patient—God isn't finished with me yet"? Pretend that your child is wearing a T-shirt with that message emblazoned on it, and every time you look at him you see the reminder. Hopefully, your prodigal will grant you time to adjust too.

Vanessa and I (Brendan) have had to work diligently to rebuild trust. At first, when Vanessa began to straighten out her life, I wasn't sure that she would stay on track. In fact, I found myself defensively looking for her mistakes. She made a few false starts to changing her life before she seemed to get it together and stabilize. One day I lapsed into a critical tone as I interrogated Vanessa about why she only attended church on the weekends that she had custody of her son. She immediately looked at me with those beautiful green eyes and said, "Mom, do you understand why I can't come on those weekends? I have to work." In an instant I realized that I was viewing Vanessa as the prodigal she had been, not as the mature young woman she had become. I grabbed Vanessa and hugged and kissed her and said, "Honey, you have worked so hard to overcome so much. I am proud of you whether you are in church every Sunday or not." Vanessa's eyes watered and she relaxed her guard. Only a few years ago Vanessa had struggled to keep a job more than two months, and now she was a manager in a large grocery store chain, loved her job, and had stayed for two years. I thanked God for helping *her* heal her wounds from this experience. Vanessa's return is still in progress, but it *is* in progress.

CLOSE *the* EXITS

One requirement for a close relationship to thrive is that both parties agree to close the exits. With marriage, couples who have closed the exits work through conflicts by remaining together and developing communication skills. Between parent and child, the temptation to escape when things heat up is a frequent problem. Although sometimes a separation is necessary in order to cool down and regain composure, you and your prodigal must agree to stay connected (that is, to come back and work out any conflicts). The best way to do that is to talk about how the two of you are doing in the process of her return. In other words, get an eagle's viewpoint—fly over the terrain and see what the overall progress looks like.

Even though you're usually going through each encounter more like a plodding turtle, stop occasionally and discuss the big picture. Try to keep the discussion focused on the positive—what is going right? Where there are trouble spots, try to own up to your part in hopes that she will own up to hers. The emotional "stretch" involved here is that you and your child are beginning to have a truly adult-to-adult relationship instead of a parent-child exchange.

It's very important to present any unfinished feelings you have to the Lord and enlist His help in dispelling them. You cannot approach your child as an adult if you are harboring resentment or memories of the less-than-adult things he has done in the past. The goal is to be in a place where you can extend to your child the unconditional love of the father demonstrated in Jesus' parable. You want to be able to gladly set out the robe, the ring, and the sandals.

Identify any exits you tend to take when feeling stressed by relationships or circumstances. Some people shut down, withdraw, and feel sorry for themselves. Others attack with criticism or act out indirectly by overeating, oversleeping, overspending, or "over" doing in some way. If your prodigal senses that you are not going to react the way you always did in the past, she will be more likely to respond differently too. It may take a few trials to completely close the exits, but keep at it. You've run the marathon of praying through this ordeal; don't quit so near the finish line.

PRAYER *Starter*

Visualize your child walking toward you with a humble look on her face. Praise God for the miracle of a changed life. Imagine setting out the robe, the sandals, and the ring. Ask God to reveal which symbolic acts would most deeply etch His love on your child's heart.

PRAYER STRATEGIES

Surrendered heart: Are you harboring any grudges toward your prodigal?

Faith-builder: Believe that your child is coming back because your love is what he needs. Trust God to show you how to restore that closeness.

Persistent prayer: If there ever was a time to pray, it is now. Your child is terrified to return. Pray for peace in everyone's heart.

Written prayer: Write what comes to mind when you think about the robe, the sandals, and the ring.

Shared prayer: Invite your praying friends to celebrate with you and to lay hands on you as you begin the mission of reconciliation.

Chapter 16

RECONCILING

THE PERSON WHO MOVES A MOUNTAIN BEGINS BY
CARRYING AWAY SMALL STONES.
—CHINESE PROVERB

You've achieved the goal of seeing your prodigal return; now you face another set of challenges. How will you navigate the gulf of differences between the prodigal and everyone else? To *reconcile* means "to bring back together, to reunite, to merge, or to patch up." All of those descriptors fit.

Mary Robinson, United Nations High Commissioner for Human Rights and former president of Ireland, said in an interview published in *O* magazine, "There's a wonderful expression that I used a lot when I was president of Ireland: It is in each other's shadow that we flourish. This means that when we stay near one another and help one another in times of trouble, we can heal."[1] You and your prodigal are just beginning the next leg of this arduous journey, and the road to reconciliation requires a toll. The toll is to surrender your defenses and work in each other's shadow until reconciliation is achieved.

Reconciliation is one of the deepest, most profound experiences in any relationship. It asks us to lay down our tried-and-true defenses and seek forgiveness of each other. Surely we all enter such a sacred connection with a sense of inadequacy. No matter how much you've longed for this opportunity you will find the task akin to docking a satellite in a space station. It looks easy, but it took a whole team of NASA experts years of preparation to pull it off. Just remember that you and your family have the greatest Expert of all on your team.

Reunion GRIEF

There is a psychological phenomenon called "reunion grief." The term refers to the strange tendency of humans to have difficulty receiving the thing they have most longed for, but learned to live without. For example, when a person who has been starved is given food, the body may throw up the first bites because it had adapted to living without food, and introducing food shocks the system. Another example is the reaction of an adult whose parent gets sober after years of drunkenness. The adult child of the recovering alcoholic is both pleased to see his parent stop drinking and enraged that it took so long. Accepting the newly reformed family member feels more like an insult than a reason to celebrate.

When your family reunites, don't be surprised if you find yourself reacting with unexpected hostility. You may be elated to have the chance to reconcile with your child yet not know what to do with the anxiety and hurt that have accumulated over the time she was gone. Fellowship with each other may require learning to relax when you're together. If your family is large, the dynamics are even more complex.

Pray that God will heal the resentments and open the pathways for each of you to accept the other's efforts to relate, no matter how awkward or untimely. Pray that the pain of reunion will not surpass the hope of a new direction.

FORGIVENESS

Without launching into a lengthy expository on the subject, let's focus on the kind of forgiveness required of a parent when his prodigal returns. Most people believe that forgiveness is impossible unless the offender admits her offense. Another variation is that we cannot forgive unless the offender repents and turns away from the sinful behavior or attitude that has caused the problem. Still others insist that we should be in a position of willingness to forgive regardless of whether the offender ever repents. Each point of view makes sense.

Assuming that your child has turned around and at least begun the journey back to a relationship with God and with you, the process of forgiveness must begin. Your prodigal may have false starts or may stumble or regress. However, if her basic desire is to repent, return, and reconcile, then you are faced with practicing the approach Jesus laid out in Matthew 18:21-22. When Peter asked Jesus how many times we should be expected to forgive someone who has sinned against us, he was shocked by the answer. Jesus said, "Seventy times seven!" In other words, Jesus expects us to forgive (and keep forgiving) people, no matter how many times we've been injured. If you can't tell what your prodigal's intentions are or you are stuck in your own reactions, then you are faced with an emotional crisis.

THE CRISIS OF FORGIVENESS

Author and *Walk in the Word* radio Bible teacher James MacDonald gave the best explanation of forgiveness we've heard. He says that forgiveness happens when:

> I make the choice to release a person from the obligation that resulted when he or she injured me; . . . I am not looking for vengeance; I am not trying to get even; I am not wishing for

bad things to happen to them; and I am not focused on their failure. In fact, I am not thinking about them at all. I've released them from all obligation that resulted when they hurt me.

MacDonald goes on to delineate a difference between the *crisis of forgiveness* and the *process of forgiveness.* The *crisis* of forgiveness is when you grapple with a basic decision to forgive or not. The *process* of forgiveness results in these actions:

1. I won't bring the offense up to the *person,* except for his benefit;
2. I won't bring the offense up to *others;* and (hardest of all)
3. I won't bring the offense up to *myself.* I will not go over it and think about it and dwell on it.[2]

MacDonald suggests that sometimes we may be working on the process but have to cycle back into the crisis stage, repeating the basic decision-making work if we realize that we are holding grudges or unforgiveness. With prodigal children the "obligatory debt" may be immense. Parents may have to decide to forgive more than once.[3]

The PRICE of UNFORGIVENESS

In her book *The Power of a Praying Parent,* Stormie Omartian writes:

> Forgiveness is a choice you make. . . . If you don't forgive, it brings death into your life in one form or another. The best way to become forgiving is to pray for the person you need to forgive. . . . We have observed firsthand, as we're sure you have, families who wait for forgiveness to happen. They don't forgive until they feel like forgiving. As a result, there are often serious rifts among family members. . . . A distinct lack of graciousness and mutual appreciation undergirds every word and deed because a spirit of unforgiveness has been

given a home there. A whole family suffers when one or more of its members walk in an unforgiving stance toward one another.[4]

Unforgiveness can be a subtle facial expression, an oversight, thoughtlessness, or a lingering attitude that keeps you from opening your heart to your returning child. No matter how you try to cover it up, if you are bitter it will show. For your own sake, let it go. Actress and Bible teacher Jeanette Clift George says, "Nothing is more exhausting than bitterness. It is in itself a full-time job, requiring high maintenance, constant attention, established priority and offering neither reward nor rest."[5] You may not even recognize that you are demonstrating unforgiveness. Ask a trusted friend for his or her perspective.

One of the poignant things Vanessa told me (Brendan) after her return was that she remembered that almost every time she saw me during the period when she was at her lowest, I asked if she wanted me to pray for her. I honestly did not remember doing that. The offer didn't feel very powerful at the time, but now I realize how important it may have been. No matter how disappointed I felt with Vanessa's choices I wanted her to know that forgiveness and relationship with God were still possible. Little did I know that a small act like offering to pray for Vanessa would give her reassurance that her mother hadn't given up. We were especially touched when Vanessa offered to share her story.

VANESSA'S *Story in* HER WORDS

I left without a backward glance . . . into another world filled with guilt and depression. After a four-year marriage my husband filed for divorce. I thought I could get away from it all by using various drugs, alcohol, sleep, sex, shopping—anything in excess. I pretended everything was normal even though I stole money, made pseudo-friends, got high, and slept around. In a span of six months, I lost everything—custody of my child, my honesty, my self-respect, my family, and my relationship with God. When my husband didn't want me, I figured, "Why would anyone else?" My life was out of control.

It's almost like I had to lose control to regain it. After my car was repossessed, I was kicked out of my apartment. That led to losing all my possessions, spending the night in jail, and in the process gaining a new outlook on life. With no money left for drugs, I got sober and found a job. I slept where I could. Eventually I got up the courage to call home. That was the hardest thing of all. I didn't want to face the people I had hurt, and I was sure they would not accept me back.

One night at work I mustered enough nerve to make the call. When Mom said she wanted me home, I was startled. Even though I was sure that I didn't deserve forgiveness or help, I kept having this nudging feeling that I should ask. Not everyone has to hit rock bottom, but I never want to come that close again. When I moved back home I was determined to prove myself worthy, and that took three years to accomplish. Now I enjoy being honest with myself and with others. I especially enjoy spending quality time with my son. And it's great to have a good relationship with Christ. His forgiveness is the most important of all.

Unconditional love comes in many forms. Sometimes God nudges my conscience until I do what is right. Sometimes just feeling the innocent love of my child reminds me that I am loved. The love of a patient and forgiving parent goes a long way.

With God's help all things are possible. He protected, guided, and forgave me when I didn't even know I needed it.

RECONCILIATION *Takes* TIME

In *How to Pray for Your Children,* Quin Sherrer tells us that forgiveness is a process that requires time for our emotions to come into agreement with the decision we have made. This takes longer for some than for others, but once we decide to take the first step toward forgiveness, we can depend on God's strength to help us continue the process. The following elements are part of this process:

- Giving up the desire to punish or get even
- Excusing for a fault or offense
- Turning from defensiveness
- Ceasing to feel resentment
- Renouncing anger
- Absolving from payment[6]

Forgiveness is such a stretch for most of us. Let's face it; we're not good at letting go. I (Brendan) have seen so many clients who struggled with the need to give their loved one a second (or twentieth) chance, saying, "I just can't forget what she did." Staying stuck in protest over the hurts your prodigal has caused you will not get you the peace or joy you want. Releasing your resentments not only frees your child to start again, but it also releases you from the bondage of hatred and fear. Of course you have no guarantee that your prodigal won't cause heartache again, but without an opportunity to live her life differently in love and acceptance, what chance does she have? Get unstuck from your protest. Give her the freedom to become a godly person. That's what Jesus did for you.

The other side of the forgiveness coin is seeking forgiveness from your prodigal for any of *your* actions that hurt her or contributed to her rejection of God. Here's where we separate the men from the boys in the parent pool. We are naturally inclined to believe that our child has hurt us and ruined our lives rather than looking at the reality that relationships are a two-way street. Although (as discussed in an earlier chapter) occasionally parents do everything right but their child still rebels, most of the time parents have contributed to the problem at some point along the way. Either the parent pressured the child, neglected the child, or somehow created an insecure attachment; these are dynamics that generally produce defiant, wounded children who seek love in self-destructive ways.

Throughout the New Testament Jesus gives the same instruction over and over: *Forgive others because you too have sinned.* He doesn't ask us to magnanimously stoop and forgive the poor wretches who are not as righteous as we are. We think Jesus wants us to understand how similar we all are, not how different. Yet again and again in my (Brendan's) practice I watch clients struggle to admit, "I hurt you when I said that." Those are simple but powerful words! As the defensive one admits her flaws, the pain melts away from the face of the other. Suddenly it's as if they are on the same team, enemies no more. That's what we want to achieve with our prodigals. The only way they will ever believe our forgiveness of them is if we demonstrate the willingness to confess our own sins.

A *Family* RESTORED: CURTIS'S *Story*

"I'm never gonna like that man. You shouldn't have married him. He's the reason you divorced my dad. Don't even ask me to treat him with respect because it ain't gonna happen," Curtis fumed. He'd been out drinking with his buddies and he always had more courage to mouth off to his mother when he had a few beers in him. Doris, Curtis's mother, stood at the kitchen island chopping onions, crying for more reasons than the pungent fumes. She'd raised Curtis as an equal, not as a child. He was the only boy in the family, and Doris had grown up thinking men had all the power. Now she was dealing with a son who had all the power and no respect for her feelings or for himself. Seventeen years old, he'd been selling drugs, getting in fights with dangerous characters in seedy places, and drinking heavily. School was something he did when it suited him. Basically, he ran the show. And what a show!

When Hank, Curtis's new stepfather, attempted to enforce discipline with Curtis, Curtis pulled out all the stops. He escalated his bad behavior until Doris and Hank decided to send Curtis to a residential treatment program in a remote Western state. They prayed about Curtis's cooperation and ultimately had to hire a six-foot-four bodyguard to accompany him on the plane.

After four months in the wilderness with round-the-clock counseling, Curtis faced his resentments and hurts. He opened up to the staff and began to mature. When he returned home, he was willing to accept his stepfather, but stepping down from equality with his mother was harder. It was hard for Doris too. The adjustment took months, with regular supportive counseling and lots of friends praying for the family.

"You know, I don't like not getting to be the man of the house, but I guess it just has to be that way," mused Curtis as he sat in the counselor's office.

"I'm really proud of the way you decided to work with your mom and stepdad instead of doing everything you could to make them miserable," his counselor observed.

"Yeah, well, sitting out in the middle of nowhere for four months made me appreciate them more. But sometimes when Hank gives me a certain look, I still want to deck him."

Smiling at his bluntness the counselor said, "God wants you to find a way to be part of your family and to help your family grow."

Curtis pulled on his cap and mumbled, "Yeah, I know."

Curtis's parents rescued him from his own self-destructive impulses by getting help for him. And, thankfully, he responded to the opportunity; not all interventions work. Several years later, Curtis called his counselor to tell her that he had gone to college and was planning to go into business with his stepfather. He added that the road to family reconciliation had been bumpy at times, but they all knew when to stop reacting and to sit down and talk about the tension. He had finally been able to forgive his mother for divorcing his father and remarrying. And his mother had apologized for expecting him to make such a huge transition too quickly. Healing takes time.

PRAYER *Starter*

Think in terms of God's time. He has all the time in the world to bring about reconciliation. Ask Him to give you a sense of having all the time you need.

Pray the Prayer of St. Francis of Assisi:

> Lord, make me an instrument of your peace. Where there is hatred, let me sow love; where there is injury, pardon; where there is doubt, faith; where there is despair, hope; where there is darkness, light; where there is sadness, joy. O Divine Master, grant that I may not so much seek to be consoled as to console; to be understood as to understand; to be loved as to love. For it is in giving that we receive; it is in pardoning that we are pardoned; and it is in dying that we are born to eternal life. Amen.

PRAYER STRATEGIES

Surrendered heart: Be the first one to admit your wrongs and make amends.

Faith-builder: Look for the signs of transformation in yourself as well as in your child. Give God the glory.

Persistent prayer: Ask yourself whether you believe that God will finish a good work that He has started. If you believe that, keep praying for completion of the work He has begun.

Written prayer: Write the obstacles to reconciliation as you see them. Pray over each one and ask God to remove them.

Shared prayer: Ask three people to pray that God will bind up the Enemy so that he cannot attack what your family is building.

Dear Prodigal:

The honor of your presence is requested at a great feast
to celebrate the fulfillment of
God's plan for your life.

Your parents will be sitting with you
at the head table.
Presents will be provided by the
Great High God, Emmanuel,
King of Kings,
Lord of Lords.

The festivities begin as soon as you arrive.

Chapter 17

HIS SPLENDOR FOR
YOUR CHILD

WHO ELSE AMONG THE GODS IS LIKE YOU, O LORD?
WHO IS GLORIOUS IN HOLINESS LIKE YOU—
SO AWESOME IN SPLENDOR,
PERFORMING SUCH WONDERS?
—EXODUS 15:11

Your prodigal has returned. The intense worry is behind you but now you live with the knowledge that your child is capable of turning his back on God again. Before he left for the "far country" of lies and defeat, you enjoyed a naïve hope that your child would live happily ever after. Now you live with a different kind of hope. It's the kind of hope that has withstood the tests of rebellion and disconnection. You and your prodigal have personally tasted God's love and forgiveness. You've been transformed. Now it's kingdom time. Time for the banquet, and you don't want to miss a thing.

The God of the universe has prepared a table stacked with beautiful gifts that have your child's name on them. You approach the array of gifts in awe. How incredible that He kept all those blessings until your child was ready to accept the invitation. It's like a surprise party held in your child's honor. Your son or daughter had no idea that God had all of this planned just for him or her. You may be thinking something like the psalmist when he wrote,

> O Lord my God, you have done many miracles for us.
> Your plans for us are too numerous to list.
> If I tried to recite all your wonderful deeds,
> I would never come to the end of them. (Psalm 40:5)

Obviously, the preparations going on behind the scenes were enormous!

Why ARE WE *So* SURPRISED *by* HIS SPLENDOR?

Nature produces daily evidence that a mighty, creative God exists who designed every detail of this world. The panoply of stars at night, the colors of a sunset, the intricacies of a spider web, and the brilliant green of tree leaves after a storm all declare His splendor. Yet we ignore the signs. We choose to believe the lie that God doesn't exist, isn't interested, or isn't worth knowing.

When your prodigal started out on his journey he probably schemed and imagined ways to be god: Take control. Don't let them push you around. You know what you need. Such are the enticing messages that Satan whispers in the soon-to-be-prodigal's ear, messages of false hope and the illusion of power. Compared to all those inflated shallow promises, God's way seemed dull and tedious. Why would anyone want to take the hard way when he could get where he wanted to go much faster? It's because he didn't know about the banquet. It's one of those things you have to witness with your own eyes. And the eyes of the prodigal setting out for the far country are turned the wrong direction. She just can't see the awesomeness of God.

I (Brendan) once attended a retreat for seventh graders held at a campground/conference center I had never previously visited. I got up early the first morning and set out looking for a cup of coffee. Being somewhat directionally challenged, I took off through the woods in the direction I thought would take me to the dining hall. After hiking five miles, I finally arrived, huffing and puffing, at the dining hall in severe caffeine withdrawal. One of the camp counselors walked up and explained that I had been only a few yards from the dining hall when I began, but I had gone in the opposite direction. I was not a happy camper!

The Israelites wandered in the wilderness for forty years when they could have made it to the Promised Land in eleven days if they had listened to God's directions. Instead, they wanted to do it their way. They suffered the consequences of stubbornness. Your child didn't believe that what God offered was good enough because the world told her it wasn't. Satan's messages appeal to our weakness. Satan can wrap his ugly surprises in some very attractive packages. Your child had to feel the emptiness of Satan's gifts before appreciating the value of God's.

How LONG WILL *the* BANQUET *Be* AVAILABLE?

As long as it takes your child to get there, the banquet table will be set and ready. Your fear tells you otherwise, but you must not give up. As long as your child is breathing, he or she has another chance to attend. God is inclusive, not exclusive. He wants every one of us at His banquet. He personally selected each of our gifts—love, acceptance, peace, abundant joy, talents, and opportunities.

God wanted your child to enjoy His inheritance without ever needing to leave "home." He provided an "express" ticket that would have allowed her to arrive early and stay longer. She could have been enjoying the party all this time. But she refused the express pass. Eventually she came to realize that the "far country" was not where her fulfillment was to be found. In his book *Experiencing Spiritual Breakthroughs,* Bruce Wilkinson writes about "the geography of change," saying, "Your life is neither a steady growth line nor an endless plateau. . . . In fact, the Lord delights to bring us to these breakthrough points where an intense desire to overcome or change runs smack up against a wall of resistance."[1]

Over and over in Scripture we read that God is patient with us when we struggle with disbelief or disobedience. Anthony Simmons, pastor of Faith Baptist Mission in Houston, tells his congregation, "We have a God who sits high and reaches low." Pastor Simmons knows the redeeming love of the Savior firsthand. He was a prodigal. Incarcerated in the Texas prison system four times, he spent most of his early adult life behind bars. Interestingly, he had a praying mother and grandmother who never gave up hope. God penetrated Simmons's faulty thinking while he lay on a hard, flat prison bunk, and he went to his knees, asking Jesus to take his life and use it. From that day, he immersed himself in God's Word and ministered to anyone who would listen. When he was released from prison, a pastor friend and mentor invited him to church. Anthony arrived eager to serve, becoming involved in every part of church ministry. A few years later his mentor died and the church unanimously voted for Anthony to take over as spiritual leader.

Today his small church has a large impact on the surrounding community. He has become one of God's most faithful and committed servants. When he goes back into the prisons to share his testimony and his story of God's redemptive power, the inmates hang on every word. Many ministers bring a similar message, but few of them have the impact of Anthony Simmons. This disobedient, rebellious prodigal is now proof that God is compassionate and merciful. Yes, your child can still claim the blessings that come from above, no matter when he arrives. Our God is compassionate and merciful.

WHAT *If* MY CHILD *Relapses?*

Prodigals sometimes sabotage their recovery. As with the "reunion grief" mentioned in the last chapter, your child's emotional readiness for change may not be a straight path. He may react negatively to the blessings if he isn't sure he deserves them or doesn't yet trust God completely. People who have suffered disillusionment and low self-esteem tend to have difficulty holding a blessing. It's almost as if their spirits are like sieves: as quickly as blessings come into their lives they lose or forget them and return to the familiar feelings of alienation and despair.

If your child relapses, keep praying. Don't give up. Plead your child's case before God. You want your child at the banquet and so does God. Pray that she will recognize the value of God's gifts. Ask the Holy Spirit to intercede in ways you cannot perceive. Read this Scripture and put your child's name in the spots where it fits:

> He is the Holy Spirit, who leads [your child's name] into all truth. The world at large cannot receive him, because it isn't looking for him and doesn't recognize him. But [your child's name] does, because he lives with [your child's name] now and later will be in [your child's name]. No, I will not abandon [your child's name] as an orphan—I will come to [your child's name]. (John 14:17-18)

Pray for your child to be able to hold the blessings God gives. Ask the Lord to open your child's eyes to the abundance and to eliminate any distortion in your child's perceptions.

BANQUET *Time!*

If your child has made breakthroughs in her life and is seeking a lasting relationship with God, it's time to celebrate. Your prayers have paid off. Now you and your family get to step from the dark hallway outside into the banquet hall and see the glorious decorations. Have you ever redecorated a room? Remember how excited you were when you saw the beautiful accessories, like the colorful, handwoven throw pillows? The details made the room come to life. Imagine the banquet hall decorated in the style of ancient extravaganzas. People would be sitting around the room on giant overstuffed pillows made of fine fabrics.

Pillows bring to mind lots of wonderful imagery. We use them to prop ourselves up when we need support. There are travel-sized pillows, corrective pillows, pillows that are original works of art. Ring bearers in weddings carry the ring, a symbol of commitment, on a velvet pillow as they approach the altar. A room without pillows looks empty and sterile. The banquet hall of the King is certainly not empty or sterile. Imagine walking into this great room decorated in whatever style feels right. Take in the beauty.

REASON *to* CELEBRATE: STACY'S *Story*

Stacy's mother walked out on their family when Stacy was a baby. Her father did the best he could as a single parent to take care of his three children. When Stacy was five years old, an angel named Inez came into her life. Stacy thought Inez was an angel because she was willing to raise someone else's children. By the time Inez married Stacy's dad, Stacy easily called her "Mom." For a few years the blended family functioned like a "normal" family. They went on vacations, attended church, and for a while it seemed as though they would live happily ever after.

Unfortunately, it wasn't that easy. Stacy's stepbrother decided to live with his father, and her older sister quit school her senior year. Stacy didn't like being left behind. She began to rebel, arguing and acting out. She lied to her parents and drank a lot. Even though she had had a good relationship with her stepmother, she was bitter about her natural mother leaving. Her heart was hard and she wouldn't let anyone get close for fear they would leave too. She could see the hurt and disappointment in her stepmother's eyes but she didn't want to be smothered. Stacy took Inez's concern and advice as nagging. When Inez had surgery, Stacy "abandoned" her stepmother by leaving for a week in Florida instead of staying to help. Stacy's conscience bothered her but she just didn't want to change. She had to get away.

She moved to another city where a friend invited her to attend a church retreat. Exhausted from avoiding and running from real relationships, Stacy went to the retreat, not knowing what to expect. She met Jesus there. From that point on, her life began to change.

Stacy wasn't sure what her stepmom would think, but Inez knew that Stacy was searching and she encouraged her. The family rift began to heal. When Stacy married, both her father and her stepmother walked her down the aisle. Surrounded by her family's love, she thanked God for providing her with a mom and a dad. Though she would never understand how her natural mother could have left three little daughters, she vowed that if God allowed her to become a mother, she would give the kind of love shown by her "angel."

Not long ago, Stacy watched the friend who introduced her to Christ give birth to a daughter. She was overwhelmed by the instant bond and love she saw between mother and child. Her friend was DeEtte's daughter, Layne.

Stacy experienced the long road from rebellion to healing. She will be seated in a place of honor at the banquet. And her parents will be there too. As will Layne.

LAYNE'S *Story* IN HER *Own* WORDS

As I look back at the stage of my life when *I* knew what was best, and things were on *my* timetable, I realize how lost I really was.

Everything in my life was based on what felt good at that moment. I didn't care about the consequences I would face as a result of my carefree attitude. I didn't believe any of the decisions I made affected anyone else. I was living for me.

My relationship with my mother and father was very strained. Time after time I found myself lying to them because I knew they wouldn't approve of me or of my actions. As each lie grew bigger and bigger, it was harder to remember what I had actually told them so I wouldn't get caught.

Each Sunday morning my mother would beg me to go to church, but partying on Saturday night was more important. Who wanted to go to church with a hangover? Every time my mother mentioned the name "God" or told me how she was "praying" for me, I would roll my eyes and smirk. I think she could tell even over the phone.

I wanted to have a special relationship and closeness with my parents but it seemed as though we had nothing in common. I recall a phone conversation when we agreed to just talk about the weather and current events to avoid real life issues. How shallow I had become.

In 1997 I was planning to be married because I thought it might be a good time to grow up. I asked my fiancé to attend church with me. An article in the paper said that Chuck Swindoll was preaching nearby. Of course, we were late so we had to sit high in the balcony. Regardless, his words reached me. He asked the simple question, "Look back at yourself over the past year. Do you like who you see?"

From that moment my life began to change. I sobbed for hours and my fiancé had no idea what was happening. He didn't understand. When I told him, he said he liked me as I was. Why didn't I?

God started pulling the strings of my heart and I found myself at a friend's doorstep. I asked, "What do I do now?" She said, "If you choose to respond to God's call, everything in your life will be different."

I began to change and so did the relationship with my fiancé. He didn't like who I was becoming. He missed the old me; I didn't. The relationship ended. I was devastated but now turned toward God and my parents. I concentrated on healing and strengthening these connections. The love and comfort of my mom and the reflection of God in my parents carried me through this difficult time.

Soon after, I got honest with my parents about who I had been and what I had been doing. I had no idea how much pain I caused them, yet they opened their arms and welcomed me home. The prodigal child had returned.

I found a warm, loving, Bible-teaching church and became very involved. I developed my relationship with God and life became easier. Before long, I met and married a wonderful, godly man my parents adore (I forgot to mention, they never liked any of the others).

The next Christmas my mother gave me a special gift. It was a small hand-made pillow made of beautiful antique laces and ribbon. She'd had it especially embroidered with a message from her that said, "His Splendor for My Child." She told me that this had been her prayer for me, that God would reveal His best.

Today I hold His splendor in my arms. My daughter is eight weeks old. When I hold Jennifer I think of how my life could have turned out. I think of what I would have missed. Every day I am amazed by God's grace. I feel so unworthy. I turned my back on God, betrayed Him, and He turned around and blessed me a hundred times over. I am overwhelmed with gratitude. I live in His splendor!

A CHOICE *to* MAKE

We don't know whether your son or daughter will return. We don't know how your prodigal will respond to God's invitation to His splendid banquet of joy and abundant life. But we do know that He will help you deal with whatever happens. Be confident that He will go before you, behind you, and beside you on the journey. You are called to authentically reflect God's splendor in your actions and on your face, with the hope that your son or daughter will find it irresistible and want to return.

In his song "Living for the Lord," recording artist Steve Wiggins sings the poignant question, "What will Jesus say about the lives we lived? Did we soar or did we sink?"[2] You must choose how this difficult experience will change you. It *will* change you. The Lord assures us that as believers we will not grieve in the manner of those with no hope (see 1 Thessalonians 4:13). Our hope is based on the absolute love and forgiveness of Jesus Christ.

We pray that you will celebrate victory with your child. Regardless of the outcome, let this time in your life be one of emotional and spiritual growth and maturity. As the winds of disappointment attempt to drive you against the cliff of despair, climb onto the wings of our sovereign God and soar.

Appendix A:

QUIET TIME STRATEGIES

In addition to the prayer ideas given in the text of this book, we have written some reflections you can use to go deeper. Set aside a time that is sacred and secure to do these exercises. Make sure that the phone is turned off and others respect your quiet space. Prepare yourself by getting physically comfortable. Make a cup of coffee or tea and wear comfy clothes that allow you to relax. If you enjoy background music, play instrumental music softly. Select one of the reflections (we recommend that you do only one at a sitting).

Take a few breaths that are deeper than normal, particularly focusing on exhaling. Exhale very slowly through your mouth and notice the way your circulation changes slightly. You may experience a tingling in your hands or a warming throughout your body. Whatever sensations you experience, just allow your body to relax.

Now choose one of the following exercises. The more time you give to the reflection, the more opportunity there is to hear the urging of the Holy Spirit. So take all the time you want and go a little slower than you might ordinarily. Read the suggestions and pause after each thought to contemplate its meaning. Keep a notebook handy to record any insights.

HANDS

Rise in the night and cry to your God. Pour out your hearts
like water to the Lord; lift up your hands to him; plead for
your children as they faint with hunger in the streets.
(Lamentations 2:19, TLB)

The Fist

Stretch your hand in front of you on the table or on your lap.
Squeeze your hand into a tight fist and observe the sensations in
your hand, forearm, and shoulder. Feel the tension running
through your body as this one part of you tightens. Now, shake
your fist in the air as if you were expressing anger at your prodigal
for all the trouble he or she has brought into your life. Listen for
the dialogue in your head as you hear yourself telling your prodigal how mad you are. What does your prodigal say or do in
response? Be aware of how long you want to shake your fist or how
quickly your arm tires. Does this action feel powerful or futile?
What do you feel about that?

Make your hand into a fist again, but imagine that you are grab-
bing hold of your son or daughter tightly and trying not to let go.
Feel his shirt in your hand, or her hand in yours. Feel your prodigal
struggling with you to get free. Become aware of your inner reactions.
Do you feel muscles tightening in your body? Is your stomach or jaw
tensing? What do you think your prodigal sees on your face? Now let
go and *feel the separation*. Feel the emptiness where once there was
tension. What does that feel like?

Release the tension in your hand and flex the muscles. Breathe
deeply again and relax. Then open your hand and close your eyes.
Extend your hand in front of you as if you were waiting for someone to place something in your hand or remove something from it.
Ask God to show you what you need—removing, replacing, or
both.

Wringing Hands

Put both hands in front of you in your lap or on the table. Wrap them around each other as if you were washing your hands. Begin to imagine the worry that you feel at times and start wringing your hands in a more pressured manner. Notice the sensations created by this action. Where do you feel tension in your body? What thoughts come to mind? Recall a time recently when you were scared for your child and remember what went through your mind as you worried. Did you search your mind for what to do or ask why this had happened? Did you just repeat a phrase over and over, like "O God"?

Continue wringing your hands as you contemplate how much energy is being sapped from your body by this single action. Think about all the wasted energy, time, money, and sleep both you and your prodigal have spent. Begin to slow the motion from a frenzied type of movement to a deliberate, careful washing motion. Pretend that you are washing your hands and you open them slightly to let a drop of liquid soap fall into the palm. Imagine that the soap is coming from heaven and it smells so fresh. The "soap" represents hope sent from God to ease your fears. Rub your hands together gently as if you were using the soap to cleanse them. Think of the fear being washed away. Then gently move your hands across your face, simulating the motions of washing your face. Run your hands over the top of your head and around the backs of your ears. Feel the renewed energy warming your face. Thank God for the cleansing power of His love and for the hope of His presence.

Clinging Hands

Place a pillow in your lap and wrap your arms around the pillow, holding it close to your chest. Place your cheek on the pillow and imagine that you are clinging to the highest branches of a sturdy tree during a flood. Listen to the water rushing past at your feet and feel the safety and support of the tree. Feel the wind blowing your hair as you hold on for dear life. Notice what you are experiencing in that scene. Are you scared or relieved? Is it difficult to trust the tree to hold you? Can you see your hands, or do you just feel them? If you were in a flood situation like that, what would you be thinking?

Now, imagine that the tree is suddenly transformed into Jesus. You are clinging to the Rock of Ages, and His roots are deeper than any tree's. He is immovable, the safest place to be in any storm or flood. Let yourself feel humble and thankful for His strength when you are weak. Picture Him holding you, picking you up, and carrying you to higher ground. As He plants your feet on the ground, notice how long it takes you to stop shaking. Ask Him to go back and rescue your prodigal too. Listen to His reply.

Read the words of this song and reflect on your responses.

> When my burden's heavy
> I shall not be moved.
> When my burden's heavy
> I shall not be moved.
> Just like a tree that's planted near the water
> I shall not be moved.
> —Traditional spiritual

Waving Hands

Wave your hand in the air as if you were waving to someone who is approaching. Imagine that the "someone" is your lost child walking up the road. Wave your hands to signal him that you are there waiting. Do you run to him? Do you start jumping for joy? Feel the exhilaration of seeing your child returning to faith. Pay attention to your hands and what they do naturally—waving, reaching, hugging. Let the joy wash over you. "I will bless you as long as I live, lifting up my hands to you in prayer" (Psalm 63:4, TLB).

FEET

You have made a wide path for my feet
to keep them from slipping. (2 Samuel 22:37)

He lifted me out of the pit of despair,
out of the mud and the mire.
He set my feet on solid ground
and steadied me as I walked along. (Psalm 40:2)

Quaking Feet

Sit in a chair and take off your shoes. Place both feet on the floor and look at them. Recall all the expressions related to feet and fear—for example, "cold feet" or "feet of clay." Imagine that you are scared and your feet are trembling. You may feel it internally or you may actually see your feet shake. Either way, pretend that your feet can talk to you. Pause and consider what they would say about what is happening with your prodigal. What might your feet tell you they want you to do? Contemplate the answers to those questions.

Read 2 Samuel 22:34. Think about a mountain goat's amazing ability to climb craggy mountain terrain without falling. Ask God to give you "hinds' feet" for this journey over rocky terrain.

Feet Planted Firmly

Stand in the middle of the room where you have plenty of space to spread your arms. Close your eyes for a moment and imagine that you are a great oak tree. Plant your feet solidly on the floor, then imagine that roots are shooting out through your feet into the ground, spreading wider than all your branches. Now feel a strong wind blowing and notice your stability. Let yourself take in that sensation. That is the strength of the Lord. Ask Him to help you develop the kind of faith that can withstand any storm that may come.

In the next few days experiment with this imagery. Recall the feeling of being a firmly rooted tree. No matter where you are, take a few seconds and retrieve that feeling of solid faith. Use it as a resource to help you endure.

Plodding Feet

Some days you are doing well to put one foot in front of the other. Forget soaring to great heights; to keep going is good enough. These are the "plodding" days. If you're having one of those days, use this reflection.

Stand and take four steps across the room. Notice whether you stepped lightly or heavily. Back up and walk across the same space again, only this time pretend that you are walking through thick pudding. Feel the resistance and heaviness of each move. You can still move forward, but each move takes a conscious effort. Imagine that the Lord is right behind you encouraging you to not give up. He is whispering to you as you plod through, "I'm here. Keep going. You'll find a way out of this place and it will be better." Now walk across the room placing heel to toe, one step at a time. Is it more frustrating when you felt the obstacle of "pudding" or when you placed one foot down carefully before figuring out where the next step went?

Think about the path you are on. Are there obstacles that make every move difficult? Do you have to be so careful that you feel as if you're hardly making progress? Plodding along is part of the journey. In fact, it may be an important part of your journey. Don't minimize the value of any of your experiences. Let them teach you more about faith. Ask God to stay with you. Read these passages.

Mark out a straight path for your feet. Then those who follow you, though they are weak and lame, will not stumble and fall but will become strong. (Hebrews 12:13)

Make me walk along the path of your commands, for that is where my happiness is found. (Psalm 119:35)

I will teach you wisdom's ways and lead you in straight paths. If you live a life guided by wisdom, you won't limp or stumble as you run. (Proverbs 4:11-12)

Running Feet

So he returned home to his father. And while he was still a long distance away, his father saw him coming. Filled with love and compassion, he ran to his son, embraced him, and kissed him. (Luke 15:20, emphasis added)

Pray for the day when you will run to meet your prodigal as she returns. Take time now to visualize the scene. You see her in the distance; she's not all the way home. But you can't stand to wait another moment. You sprint to her, throw your arms around her, and kiss her. Your heart is so relieved! She has returned. She's not lost forever. Today, look at your feet and imagine them running down your driveway or across your yard. Feel the pavement as each stride hits the ground. Experience the distance closing. Do you want to run faster? Or are you hesitant to greet this wayward child? Maybe you're not ready yet. Ask the Lord to prepare your heart and mind to run when you see your prodigal returning.

Dancing Feet

Party time! Put some lively music on the stereo or radio and pay attention to your feet as they dance across your bedroom floor. This is not a dancing lesson; this is a celebration. Remember comedian Steve Martin's routine called "Happy Feet"? In his act he went crazy, as if his feet had a mind of their own, cavorting across the stage, jerking his body to and fro. The audience couldn't contain their laughter.

Imagine that kind of elation. It overtakes you and you have to dance. Think of the way David danced into Jerusalem when he finally became king after years of persecution and separation from his calling. Ask God for that kind of joy. You may not know when that prayer will be answered, but when it is, you'll know the steps.

HEARTS

My heart is confident in you, O God;
no wonder I can sing your praises! (Psalm 57:7)

Broken Hearts

A glad heart makes a happy face; a broken heart
crushes the spirit. (Proverbs 15:13)

Heartbreak comes when someone you love lets you down or betrays your trust. The core of confidence you had in each other cracks wide open, leaving your most vulnerable parts exposed. Prodigals don't think about this damage when they leave. Here are a few ideas for getting through those hurting times.

Get an object the size of a heart that can be broken symbolically. You might use a dinner roll or a lump of clay. Break it in two and set it in front of you. Stare at it quietly for a few minutes and think about the brokenness in your family or in your own heart. Say out loud the things that have broken your heart. Allow yourself to explore your emotional and mental responses to the brokenness. Imagine God's sadness for you and your child. Notice whether you have difficulty tolerating these thoughts. Do you want to switch subjects to avoid the pain? Are you surprised by the magnitude of the pain? Do you feel as if you can never repair the damage?

Now invite Jehovah Rapha, God Our Healer, to sit down with you. Ask Him to assess the damage and give His perspective on this broken heart of yours. Ask Him whether He is ready to heal you or not. Ask whether He wants to heal your heart. Listen quietly to His reply. Take that in. Respect the importance of timing and readiness for healing a heart. God is the greatest heart surgeon of all time. Trust Him.

Empty Hearts

> I will give them hearts that will recognize me as the Lord.
> They will be my people, and I will be their God, for they will
> return to me wholeheartedly. (Jeremiah 24:7)

An empty heart is one in which something is missing. Do you remember the first time you held your newborn? You felt as if your heart would burst, so filled was it with love and pride for that little miracle of yours. No emptiness that day. But now that baby has chosen to leave you and all you represent. There is a gaping hole where the fulfillment of dreams was supposed to be. Your heart is empty and longing for the joy and peace you once had. The emptiness aches.

Close your eyes and picture your own heart as it pumps blood to all the vital organs of your body as well as to the extremities. Place your hand on your chest over your heart. See if you can feel the beat. Sit quietly and become more and more aware of what's missing in your life. Snapshots of happier days may scroll across the screen in your mind. Let them. Those images are letting you know what you are missing most. Pay attention to the images and acknowledge that they matter to you. Tell your heart that you know it feels empty. Invite Christ to come and fill the empty places with the fruit of the Spirit. Imagine Him carefully placing gentleness, kindness, faithfulness, patience, goodness, self-control, joy, peace, and love in each chamber of your heart so that they can be dispatched to every needy part of you. Focus on the sensation of being *filled* with God's Spirit.

Resting Hearts

> He lets me rest in the meadow grass and leads me beside the
> quiet streams. He gives me new strength. He helps me do
> what honors him the most. (Psalm 23:2, TLB)

Does your heart feel weary? Wrestling with the multitude of dilemmas you face with your prodigal takes so much emotional energy.
One of the most restorative things you can do is rest. Just lie down
beside still waters and take a nap or drift off; rather than be in a
hurry to solve all the problems, just *be*. Use this exercise to renew
your strength. Remember that you are not wrestling with God; you
and God are wrestling with the problems. God wants to give you
rest. Will you accept it?

If possible, find a comfortable place on the floor or on a sofa.
Dim the lights. Play quiet, relaxing music. Prop up your head and
knees so that you can feel completely supported as you lie down for
this exercise. Take a few deeper-than-normal breaths and imagine
that you are in a beautiful place. Perhaps you remember being on a
vacation or seeing a place featured in a magazine that you wished
you could go to. Transport yourself there in your mind. You may
have selected a beach or a mountaintop. It may be cold or sunny and
warm. Whatever you choose is perfectly all right. God has created a
variety of vistas for His people to enjoy. If you tend to have allergic
reactions to the outdoors, then you can imagine floating on a cloud
or soaking in a bath. Find the most relaxing place you can imagine
and go there. Take all the time you need to experience it vividly.

Next, imagine that God has come to that place to be with you.
No pressure, just companionship the way it was in the Garden of
Eden. He is enjoying the rest too. And He's so glad to see you.
Begin telling Him what has been wearing you out lately. Imagine
Him nodding with understanding and looking into your eyes with
compassion. Then hear His gentle voice speaking these words:

"You've worked so hard. Lie down and rest. I'll watch over you while you are here. Take all the time you need." Breathe deeply and thank Him for caring so much.

Excited Hearts

> Those who plant in tears
> will harvest with shouts of joy. (Psalm 126:5)

Do you remember your heart pounding as you waited at the airport gate for the arrival of someone you hadn't seen in a long time? You stood searching the crowd of people deplaning, walking up the jetway, anxiously hoping to see the top of your loved one's head. There he was! You could hardly believe that you were finally together again. You couldn't wait to hug him and tell him all the fun plans you'd made. That's what you look forward to experiencing with your prodigal. You hope that soon your heart will be bursting with joy because you are renewing your relationship. He has returned and he wants to change. Your heart overflows with joy and relief.

Create a compelling image of achieving this reconciliation. As you do, picture you and your child with other significant family members posing for a family portrait. See the happiness on everyone's faces. Study the face of your prodigal who has returned. Imagine that your son or daughter is laughing in a relaxed, peaceful way. Appreciate the beauty of the transformation. Praise God for this miracle. And look again at the family portrait. Do you see the face of Jesus hidden in the midst?

Overflowing Hearts

> Then Hannah prayed:
> "My heart rejoices in the Lord!
> Oh, how the Lord has blessed me!

Now I have an answer for my enemies,
as I delight in your deliverance.
No one is holy like the Lord!
There is no one besides you;
there is no Rock like our God."
(1 Samuel 2:1-2)

Breathe deeply. Close your eyes and feel the air flowing into your lungs and out. Imagine that the Holy Spirit is breathing His peace and joy directly into your body and mind. Put both hands over your heart as you continue this relaxed breathing. Feel your pulse as your heart beats. Praise God for the wonder of a beating heart. Now focus on the emotions you feel. Do you feel blessed? If not, *imagine* what that would be like—to feel so blessed and happy that you can hardly stand it. Ask God to fill your heart to overflowing with His love and peace. Ask Him to sweep away anything that clutters those places in your heart and to replace unnecessary beliefs and feelings with gratitude for all He has done. Pretend you have so many blessings that your heart is overflowing. Imagine that the overflow is spreading love to everyone important to you.

Appendix B:

SCRIPTURE PRAYERS

COPING *with the* PAIN

Read these verses as if they were written for you. They were.

But you [God] desire honesty from the heart,
so you can teach me to be wise in my inmost being.
Purify me from my sins, and I will be clean;
wash me, and I will be whiter than snow.
Oh, give me back my joy again;
you have broken me—
now let me rejoice.
(Psalm 51:6-8)

Lord, you are close to the brokenhearted;
you rescue those who are crushed in spirit.
The righteous face many troubles,
but you rescue me from each and every one.
For you protect me from harm.
(Psalm 34:18-20, author paraphrase)

Apart from you [Jesus] I can do nothing.
(John 15:5, author paraphrase)

So God, you have given us both your promise and your oath. These two things are unchangeable because it is impossible for you to lie. Therefore, we who have fled to you for refuge can take new courage, for we can hold on to your promise with confidence. This confidence is like a strong and trustworthy anchor for our souls. It leads us through the curtain of heaven into your inner sanctuary. Jesus has already gone in there for us. (Hebrews 6:17-20, author paraphrase)

> Why am I discouraged?
> Why so sad?
> I will put my hope in God!
> I will praise him again—
> my Savior and my God!
> (Psalm 42:11)

> We depend on you, Lord, alone to save us.
> Only you can help us, protecting us like a shield.
> In you our hearts rejoice,
> for we are trusting in your holy name.
> Let your unfailing love surround us, Lord,
> for our hope is in you alone.
> (Psalm 33:20-22, author paraphrase)

Though you, Lord, gave me adversity for food and affliction for drink, you will still be with me to teach me. I will see my teacher with my own eyes, and I will hear a voice say, "This is the way; turn around and walk here." (Isaiah 30:20-21, author paraphrase)

"Come to me and I will give you rest—all of you who work so hard beneath a heavy yoke." (Matthew 11:28, TLB)

Give your burdens to the Lord,
and he will take care of you.
He will not permit the godly to slip and fall. (Psalm 55:22)

"But if you stay in me and obey my commands, you may ask
any request you like, and it will be granted!" (John 15:7, TLB)

You are my hiding place from every storm of life; you even
keep me from getting into trouble! You surround me with
songs of victory. I will instruct you (says the Lord) and guide
you along the best pathway for your life; I will advise you and
watch your progress. (Psalm 32:7-8, TLB)

Let him have all your worries and cares, for he is always thinking about you and watching everything that concerns you.
(1 Peter 5:7, TLB)

INTERCEDING

In these prayers, put your child's name in the blank spaces as you
pray the Scripture.

Protection

LORD, keep _____ from all evil
and preserve _____'s life.
Keep watch over_____ as (he/she) comes and goes,
both now and forever. (Psalm 121:7-8)

"I'm not asking you to take _____ out of the world,
but to keep _____ safe from the evil one." (John 17:15)

We were crushed and completely overwhelmed, and we thought we
would never live through it. In fact, we expected to die. But as a

result, we learned not to rely on ourselves, but on God who can raise the dead. And he did deliver us from mortal danger. And we are confident that he will continue to deliver _____.
He will rescue _____ because you are helping by praying for us. As a result, many will give thanks to God because so many people's prayers for _____'s safety have been answered. (2 Corinthians 1:8-11)

Humble _____ before you, God. Help _____ resist the Devil, and he will flee from (him/her). Help _____ draw close to you, and you will draw close to (him/her). (James 4:7-8)

I ask that _____ will reject perverse ideas
  and stay away from every evil. (Psalm 101:4)

Lord, please both precede and follow _____.
Please place your hand of blessing on _____'s head. (Psalm 139:5)

Repentance
And I pray that Christ will be more and more at home in _____'s heart as [he/she] trusts in him. May _____'s roots go down deep into the soil of God's marvelous love. And may _____ have the power to understand, as all God's people should, how wide, how long, how high, and how deep his love really is. (Ephesians 3:17-18)

May _____ experience the love of Christ, though it is so great _____ will never fully understand it. Then _____ will be filled with the fullness of life and power that comes from God. (Ephesians 3:19)

Let the smile of your face shine on _____, LORD.
You have given me greater joy than those who have abundant harvests of grain and wine.

Let _____ lie down in peace and sleep, for you alone, O LORD, will keep (him/her) safe. (Psalm 4:6-8)

Lord, open _____'s eyes so _____ may turn from darkness to light, and from the power of Satan to God. Then _____ will receive forgiveness for (his/her) sins and be given a place among God's people, who are set apart by faith in you. (Acts 26:18)

Gently teach _____, who opposes the truth. Perhaps you will change _____'s heart, and _____ will believe the truth. Then _____ will come to (his/her) senses and escape from the Devil's trap. For _____ has been held captive by him to do whatever he wants. (2 Timothy 2:25-26)

Give _____ singleness of heart and put a new spirit within _____. Take away _____'s heart of stone and give _____ a tender heart instead. (Ezekiel 11:19)

People who cover over their sins will not prosper. But if _____ confesses and forsakes [his/her sins], _____ will receive mercy. (Proverbs 28:13)

Return
May _____ sing of the tender mercies of the LORD forever! (Psalm 89:1)

I pray that _____ won't be impressed with (his/her) own wisdom. Instead, _____ will fear the LORD and turn (his/her) back on evil. Then _____ will gain renewed health and vitality. (Proverbs 3:7-8)

Give _____ an understanding mind so that _____ knows the difference between right and wrong. (1 Kings 3:9)

But as for _____, let (him/her) get as close to [God] as (he/she) can! Let _____ choose him and tell everyone about the wonderful ways he rescued (him/her). (Psalm 73:28, TLB)

I pray that _____won't get tired of doing what is good. That _____won't get discouraged and give up, for (he/she) will reap a harvest of blessing at the appropriate time. (Galatians 6:9)

I could have no greater joy than to hear that _____ lives in the truth. (3 John 4)

For the power of the life-giving Spirit has freed _____ through Christ Jesus from the power of sin that leads to death. (Romans 8:2)

Appendix C:

RESOURCES

ADDICTIONS

Alcoholics Anonymous
Grand Central Station
P.O. Box 459
New York, NY 10163
212-870-3400
www.aa.org

Al-Anon/Alateen
1600 Corporate Landing Parkway
Virginia Beach, VA 23454-5617
For local meeting information, call
1-888-4-AL-ANON.
www.al-anon.org

Narcotics Anonymous
P.O. Box 9999
Van Nuys, CA 91409
818-773-9999
www.na.org

ADDITIONAL WEBSITES

Cocaine Anonymous
www.ca.org

Sex Addicts Anonymous
www.sexaa.org

Sex and Love Addicts Anonymous
www.slaatws.org

Gamblers Anonymous
www.gamblersanonymous.org

Debtors Anonymous
www.debtorsanonymous.org

PARENTING

National Runaway Switchboard
3080 N. Lincoln Ave.
Chicago, IL 60657
773-880-9860
www.NRScrisisline.org

Toughlove International
P.O. Box 1069
Doylestown, PA 18901
www.toughlove.org

Moms In Touch International
www.MomsInTouch.org

PRAYER
Pray! Magazine
P.O. Box 469084
Escondido, CA 92046
1-800-691-7729
www.praymag.com

A Constant Prayer
www.aconstantprayer.com

Billy Graham Ministries
www.billygraham.org

The Brooklyn Tabernacle
www.brooklyntabernacle.org

Christian Fellowship Center
www.christianfellowshipcorner.com

Christianity Today.com
www.christianitytoday.com

Crosswalk.com
www.crosswalk.com

Gospel.com
www.gospelcom.net

Mercy Drops.com
www.mercydrops.com

Prayer Ministries International
www.pray4you.com

Prayer Needs.com
www.prayerneeds.org

Pray 911
www.pray911.com

Prayers That Avail Much
www.prayers.org

INSPIRATION
Crosswalk.com
www.crosswalk.com

Focus on the Family/
Dr. James Dobson
www.family.org

Gospelcom
www.gospelcom.net

Insight for Living/Charles Swindoll
www.insightforliving.com

The Urban Alternative/
Dr. Tony Evans
www.tonyevans.org

Upwords, Max Lucado
www.maxlucado.com

Walk in the Word/
Pastor James MacDonald
www.walkintheword.com

INTERDENOMINATIONAL
BIBLE STUDIES
Bible Study Fellowship
19001 Huebner Road
San Antonio, Texas 78258-4019
1-877-273-3228 (toll free)
www.bsfinternational.org

Community Bible Study
1765 Business Center Drive,
Suite 200
Reston, VA 20190-5327
1-800-826-1181
www.communitybiblestudy.org

Tough Love International
P.O. Box 1069
Doylestown, PA 18901
1-800-333-1069

NOTES

INTRODUCTION

1. Oswald Chambers, *My Utmost for His Highest* (Westwood, N.J.: Barbour, 1935), p. 362.
2. Ruth Bell Graham, *Prodigals and Those Who Love Them* (Grand Rapids, Mich.: Baker, 1999).

CHAPTER 2

1. H. Norman Wright, *Loving a Prodigal: A Survival Guide for Parents of Rebellious Children* (Colorado Springs, Colo.: Chariot Victor, 1999), p. 142.
2. Robert Brooks, Ph.D., and Sam Goldstein, Ph.D., *Raising Resilient Children: Fostering Strength, Hope, and Optimism in Your Child* (Chicago: Contemporary Books, 2001), p. 2.
3. Quin Sherrer with Ruthanne Garlock, *Praying Prodigals Home: Taking Back What the Enemy Has Stolen* (Ventura, Calif.: Regal Books, 2000), p. 27.
4. James MacDonald, *Walk in the Word Ministry*, excerpt from a sermon, Houston, 25 April 2002.

CHAPTER 3

1. Charles R. Swindoll, *Wisdom for the Way: Wise Words for Busy People* (Nashville: Thomas Nelson, 2001), pp. 14-15.
2. Oswald Chambers, *My Utmost for His Highest* (Westwood, N.J.: Barbour, 1935), p. 349.
3. Mother Teresa (compiled by Jaya Chalika and Edward LeJoly), *The Joy in Loving* (New York: Penguin, 1996), p. 73.
4. Bruce Larson, *What God Wants to Know: Finding Your Answers in God's Vital Questions* (San Francisco: Harper Collins, 1993), p. 23.

CHAPTER 5

1. H. Norman Wright, *Loving a Prodigal: A Survival Guide for Parents of Rebellious Children* (Colorado Springs, Colo.: Chariot Victor, 1999), p. 142.
2. John White, *Parents in Pain: Overcoming the Hurt and Frustration of Problem Children* (Downers Grove, Ill.: Intervarsity, 1979), p. 46.
3. Mike McPherson, *Parenting the Wild Child: Hope and Help for Desperate Parents* (Minneapolis: Bethany House, 2000), p. 18.

CHAPTER 6

1. Story provided by K. G. DuBay.

CHAPTER 7

1. Max Lucado, *The Applause of Heaven* (Nashville: Thomas Nelson, W Publishing Group, 1990), pp. 113-114.
2. Dean Ornish, *Love & Survival: 8 Pathways to Intimacy and Health* (New York: HarperPerennial, 1998), p. 13.

CHAPTER 8

1. John M. Schneider, Ph.D., *Finding My Way: Healing and Transformation Through Loss and Grief* (Colfax, Wisc.: Seasons, 1994), p. 15.

CHAPTER 9

1. Jim Cymbala with Dean Merrill, *Fresh Wind, Fresh Fire: What Happens When God's Spirit Invades the Heart of His People* (Grand Rapids, Mich.: Zondervan, 1997), p. 65.
2. Sandra Higley, "A Pattern for Persistence," *Pray!*, issue 28, Jan/Feb 2002, p. 33.
3. James R. Lucas, *Proactive Parenting* (Eugene, Ore.: Harvest House, 1993).
4. Dutch Sheets, *Intercessory Prayer: How God Can Use Your Prayers to Move Heaven and Earth* (Ventura, Calif.: Regal Books, 1996), p. 180.
5. Cliff Richards and Lloyd Hildebrand, *Prayers That Prevail for Your Children: A Parent's & Grandparent's Manual of Prayers* (Tulsa, Okla.: Victory House, 1994), pp. 156-171.
6. Max Lucado, *And the Angels Were Silent* (Nashville: Thomas Nelson, 1992), p. 123.

CHAPTER 10

1. Excerpt from A. Philip Parham, *Letting God* (San Francisco: Harper & Row, 1987), 19 August reading.

CHAPTER 11

1. Sara Park McLaughlin, *Meeting God in Silence: How a Time-Honored Spiritual Discipline Can Bring Meaning to Your Life* (Wheaton, Ill.: Tyndale House, 1993), pp. 32, 79.
2. Richard J. Foster and James Bryan Smith, eds., *Devotional Classics: Selected Readings for Individuals & Groups* (San Francisco: HarperCollins, 1990), p. 143.
3. Heidi Levitt, M., "Sounds of Silence in Psychotherapy: The Categorization of Client's Pauses," *Psychotherapy Research,* 2001, vol. 11, pp. 295-309.
4. Margie M. Lewis, *The Hurting Parent: Help for Parents of Prodigal Sons and Daughters* (Grand Rapids, Mich.: Zondervan, 1988), p. 152.
5. Ron Susek, "Wrestling with Eternity," *Pray!,* issue 28, Jan/Feb 2002, pp. 16-19.
6. Jonathan Graf, "Are You in Sync? God's Cosmic Clock," *Pray!,* issue 28, Jan/Feb 2002, p. 15.

CHAPTER 12

1. H. Norman Wright, *Loving a Prodigal: A Survival Guide for Parents of Rebellious Children* (Colorado Springs, Colo.: Chariot Victor, 1999), p. 21.
2. Excerpt from a sermon by Dr. David G. McKechnie, senior pastor, Grace Presbyterian Church, Houston, 31 March 2002.

CHAPTER 13

1. Mawi Asgedom, *Of Beetles and Angels: A Boy's Remarkable Journey from a Refugee Camp to Harvard* (Chicago: Megadee Books, 2001), pp. 13-14.
2. H. Norman Wright, *Loving a Prodigal: A Survival Guide for Parents of Rebellious Children* (Colorado Springs, Colo.: Chariot Victor, 1999), p. 35.
3. Charles R. Swindoll, *Hope Again: When Life Hurts and Dreams Fade* (Nashville: Thomas Nelson, W Publishing Group, 1996).
4. Audio tape of speech by Dr. Anthony Campolo.

CHAPTER 14

1. Alexander Solzhenitsyn, quoted in Charles R. Swindoll, *Wisdom for the Way: Wise Words for Busy People* (Nashville: Thomas Nelson, 2001), p. 51.
2. Louis L'Amour, quoted in *The Change-Your-Life Quote Book*, compiled by Allen Klein (New York: Portland House/Random House, 2001), p. 130.
3. Elise NeeDell Babcock, *When Life Becomes Precious: A Guide for Loved Ones and Friends of Cancer Patients* (New York: Bantam Books, 1997), p. 19.

CHAPTER 15

1. Allison Ash, *We Give Our Lives Back to You.* (Unpublished song.) Reprinted with permission.
2. Denise Glenn, *Freedom for Mothers: Five Liberating Principles for Victorious Mothering* (Sisters, Ore.: Multnomah Publishers, 1999), p. 172.
3. Max Lucado, *The Great House of God* (Nashville: Thomas Nelson, 1997), p. 54.

CHAPTER 16

1. Mary Robinson, quoted in "An Extraordinary Panel of Thinkers, Writers, and Spiritual Leaders Answer the Question: What's the Best Way to Carry On When Things Are Shaky?" *O: The Oprah Magazine*, December 2001, p. 160.
2. James MacDonald, *Seven Words to Change Your Family . . . While There's Still Time* (Chicago: Moody Press, 2002), p. 51.
3. MacDonald, p. 52.
4. Stormie Omartian, *The Power of a Praying Parent* (Eugene, Ore.: Harvest House, 1995), pp. 179-180.
5. Jeanette Clift George, *Daisy Petals* (Houston: Mover of Grace, 1997).
6. Quin Sherrer with Ruthanne Garlock, *How to Pray for Your Children* (Ventura, Calif.: Regal, 1998), pp. 153-154.

CHAPTER 17

1. Bruce Wilkinson, *Experiencing Spiritual Breakthroughs: The Powerful Principle of the Three Chairs* (Sisters, Ore.: Multnomah, 1999), p. 20.
2. Steve Wiggins, "Living for the Lord," from the *Faith That Is Real* CD (Memphis: Ardent Music, 2002).

ABOUT BRENDAN O'ROURKE

Brendan O'Rourke, Ph.D., is a licensed clinical psychologist with a heart for Christ and more than twenty years of professional experience. Dr. O'Rourke has served as Chief of the Pain Management Clinic at the Veterans Affairs Hospital-Medical Center, Houston; staff counselor of Cancer Counseling Inc. for twenty years; and consultant to the weight loss program at NRG Wellness Center in Sugar Land, Texas.

Dr. O'Rourke heals broken lives with God's help through counseling and training of leaders. In 1994, she founded *Created New*, a small-group outreach ministry at Advent Episcopal Church. She served on the equipper team for the small-group ministry at her home church, Grace Presbyterian Church, Houston.

Dr. O'Rourke believes in empowering Christians to enjoy better marriages and family life. She leads marriage and parenting seminars for businesses, schools, and churches. She has given more than a thousand presentations on these topics and more:

- Effective communication
- Trauma resolution
- Grief and loss
- Suicide prevention
- Creativity
- Marriage
- Stress management
- Christian living
- Medical psychology
- Codependency

Dr. O'Rourke is a clinical member of the American Group Psychotherapy Association and Imago Relationship International. She has appeared on numerous radio and television programs in the Houston area.

Dr. O'Rourke has written articles in the *Bakers Encyclopedia of Psychology* ("Non-Verbal Communication") and in *The Mothers' Book of Shared Experiences* ("Coping with Infant Cancer"). In addition, she authored articles in and helped create a Lenten devotional series (*Faces at the Foot of the Cross* and *When the Shouting Won*) published by Grace Presbyterian Church of Houston.

Married to Dan O'Rourke, a media producer and broadcast journalist, Dr. O'Rourke has two grown daughters, Vanessa and Natalie; a son, Devin; and a younger daughter, Chrissy. She also has a grandson, Ty.

ABOUT DEETTE SAUER

When God entered DeEtte's life, she walked out on a lucrative and successful broadcasting career in a profession that was both stress-filled and ethics-challenged. Since then she has compared her adventure with God to riding a wild mustang bareback. Total submission and her ability to just "go with it" provided an unpredictable and sometimes scary ride. DeEtte followed the Lord into a variety of pursuits, all guiding her toward an independent study program in human behavior. After completing certification studies for alcohol and drug abuse counseling, she established a chemical abuse team for a nonprofit organization dedicated to protecting abused and neglected children. In addition, she taught behavior modification classes for large corporations such as Coca-Cola Foods, Sisters of Charity Hospital, Kelsey-Seybold Health Clinics, Pennzoil, and Bayroid. Her wit and insight have delighted many local church groups as she shares her personal testimony. DeEtte is a vital force in an inner-city mission, and she regularly participates in local prison ministries. She has a heart for the disadvantaged.

DeEtte has been married more than thirty years to George Sauer, an international corporate attorney. George and DeEtte have two daughters, two sons-in-law, and four grandchildren. She is a master's swimmer, 2001 Texas champion in four events, and a bronze medalist in the 2001 National Senior Olympics.

MORE HELP FOR INVOLVED PARENTS.